Experimental Literature: A Collection of Statements

Edited by
Jeffrey R. Di Leo
and
Warren Motte

EXPERIMENTAL LITERATURE: A COLLECTION OF STATEMENTS

EDITED BY
JEFFREY R. DI LEO
AND
WARREN MOTTE

JOURNAL OF EXPERIMENTAL FICTION 77

JEF BOOKS/DEPTH CHARGE PUBLISHING
AURORA, ILLINOIS

Cover Art & Design by Nicholas Motte

ISBN 1-884097-20-0
ISBN-13 978-1-884097-20-1

ISSN 1084-547X

This volume is a special revised and expanded edition of
American Book Review 37.5 (July/August 2016) published in
celebration of its 40th anniversary with support from the
American Book Review Endowment

JEF Books/Depth Charge Publishing

The Foremost in Innovative Fiction
Experimentalfiction.com

JEF Books are distributed to the book trade by
SPD: Small Press Distribution and to the
academic journal market by EBSCO

Experimental Literature: A Collection of Statements

Contents

Introduction

On Experimental Writing
Jeffrey R. Di Leo and Warren Motte

Experimental writing sometimes gets a bad rap. Indeed, in the words of one of our contributors, it invokes "A litany of insults."

Is it because it is often put in the same category as "failed" writing? Or is it because of the demands it places on its readers and critics? Or is it something else?

Even among those whose work clearly fits the phrase "experimental writing," there is some resistance in embracing it.

Our friend, the late Raymond Federman, would cringe every time his work was described as "experimental." But when pressed to actually dub it with a general term, Federman realized that nothing better described the type of writing he championed.

Experimental writing is not the kind of thing that you find plainly labeled in a bookstore. It is largely a designation by writers for writers.

While it's true that some experiments in writing fail, so too do some succeed. Separating the failures from the successes though is no different from distinguishing the good, the bad, and the ugly in every other type of writing.

The contributors to this collection include some of the most respected experimental writers in the world.

And none of them cringes when their work is described as "experimental writing."

Each embraces the phrase in this collection and aims to help us to distance it from the unfair assumptions of its naysayers. We not only learn many interesting things about its state and position in the world of contemporary writing, but also see that it is a much more heterogeneous field than one might assume.

But this is not to say that this collection has been clear sailing from idea to execution.

The topic that we first proposed to the participants was

"Experimental Writing, Then and Now."

As it turned out, people chose to reflect far more closely on the "now" than on the "then"—which is in itself highly encouraging to those like us who care about experimental writing as a living, enduring cultural form.

The essays in this collection represent an extreme diversity of approaches to experimental writing.

The pieces contributed by those who are primarily creative writers suggest that literary experimentalism can be conceived on a very broad horizon—as broad, undoubtedly, as the horizon on which it is practiced.

The essays provided by people who are principally academics likewise adopt very different perspectives on the matter, each one invoking a different central term ("theory," for instance, or "reading" or "criticism") and deploying it as a heuristic.

Just like the insistence on the "now," that multiplicity of approach is clearly reassuring insofar as the vitality of experimentalism is concerned.

More than anything else, the essays in this collection offer a vision of experimental writing as a mosaic, wherein different tiles interrogate each other, even as they collaborate in the formation of a coherent image.

A mosaic moreover in which the interstices between the tiles are as eloquent as the tiles themselves, suggesting that any image is necessarily interrupted, and that such interruption (as Maurice Blanchot reminds us) in fact enables continuity of understanding.

It might be argued that experimental writing is like any cultural phenomenon in our time—only more so. That is, the problems that vex our culture are magnified and exaggerated for rhetorical and polemical effect in experimental writing; aesthetic gestures are never innocent, but are instead always overdetermined and at least double; the reflexive nature of art is constantly underscored and underscored again; process issues are put on display and thematized; writers cultivate, cajole, inveigle, tyrannize, lionize, and seduce their readers, turn and turn about (and sometimes in the very same breath).

Here are some of the salient vectors in that variety of

approach:

In "remixthemind," **Mark Amerika** argues that experimentalism in its richest form is a matter of dialogue and articulation, a collaboration between an artist and a beholder, a writer and a reader.

It is the productive tension between conceptual art and the artifact, between aesthetic theory and practice. Amerika emphasizes the importance of *performance* as a fundamental principle of experimentalism. He says that it is crucial to innovate, but it is also necessary to put that process of innovation on stage and cause it to perform in the work of art, regardless of genre.

Reflecting upon the experimentalist tradition in theater, **Martine Antle** reminds us that theater is *both* text and performance, and that the "unexpectedness" of performance is central to theater of any sort at all. Yet experimental theater, she argues, typically presents itself as a "theater of the moment," both in the sense that it tends to come to the fore during times of radical change, and insofar as it calls our attention—often very insistently indeed—to the very moment of performance. Whatever else it may seek to do, experimentalist theater adopts a subversive stance with regard to mainstream tradition, wagering upon our familiarity with that tradition and our willingness to see it questioned. In that perspective, it is perhaps useful to imagine experimental theater as a discourse cast in the interrogative mode rather than the declarative, a form inviting us to rethink our own notions of theater and its uses.

"Indigo" by **Charles Bernstein** is both a memorable glance backward on a long career of attempting to respond innovatively to many of the same questions about experiment and poetry as well as a glance forward to experimental poetry in an increasingly commodified, corporatized, and conservative world. As one of the founders of $L=A=N=G=U=A=G=E$, Bernstein has genealogical obligations to the movement that are impossible to escape and the source of continued interrogation and interest. But as a poet writing in dark times, the political dimensions of his work become charged with new opportunities for "invention," a term he finds more suggestive of "*knowhow* and *pragmatism* than 'experimental.'" His distinction between "invention" and "experiment," though subtle, is an important one for those who like him aim to not merely "record plaintively … what happened to them," but, following Henry David Thoreau, to record "how they have happened to the universe."

In "Being There," **R. M. Berry** characterizes literary experimentation as "the response to a problem." That problem, as the experimental writer sees it, involves the perceived exhaustion of creativity of his or her fellow writers. It is not the first time such an idea has been articulated. One thinks of John Barth's influential essay, "The Literature of Exhaustion" (1967), which in its own way set the terms for innovative fiction in its time. Writing half a century after Barth, R. M. Berry feels that the most fundamental vocation of experimental fiction involves the discovery of what fiction actually *is*. Moreover, it is through its close focus on that question that one can recognize experimental fiction, and differentiate it from other kinds of writing: "experimental fiction," he argues, "differs from more widely recognized ways of writing by forcing the question of what fiction is."

Timothy Bewes tells about his experience of teaching a class entitled "Recent Experiments in American Fiction," hoping that it would inspire him to write the piece that appears here. It is perhaps less an anecdote than a parable; and anyone who has grappled with thorny problems in a classroom setting will certainly recognize its pungency. For Bewes, the particularity of experimental fiction resides in the notion of scandal, and more especially still "the scandal that fiction introduces into presence." For fiction is fundamentally disruptive in his view; it destabilizes the discourses with which it comes into contact; it causes us to question things we thought we knew; it makes the familiar a bit stranger than it might have seemed. Bewes grapples, too, with the language of criticism, fretting that his own remarks will betray the radical quality of the scandal that he detects. "I wanted my statement to do justice to the scandal," he writes. "The problem was that the scandal was incompatible with the composition and dissemination of any such statement."

The analogy that **Christian Bök** asks us to consider in the second of his "Statements" deals both with where we've been and where we may be going. "What *Fountain* by Marcel Duchamp has become for artists of the last century, the space-probe Voyager 1 by NASA is going to become for artists of the next century," he contends. Going forward, thus, he urges poets to be irresponsible, to put things into play, to court risk, and to dismiss any attempt to civilize or otherwise curtail those gestures with a magisterial reminder that the poem is, in the first instance, the poet's own. His brief is thus for a deeply subjectivist work of art, one that addresses a lack in the world. "I write poetry," Bök declares, "not because I feel innately 'creative' or innately 'artistic,' but because no other poet in the world seems to be writing the kind of book that I might want to read."

Different kinds of experiments are very much on the mind of **Julie Carr** in "Just Try." She points toward certain recent social experiments: tax cuts for the wealthy, for instance; cuts in federal housing assistance for the poor; the staggering—and largely unaddressed—rise in gun deaths; the prison population explosion that we are currently witnessing. She feels that she must somehow account for those types of experiment in her own practice of poetry, and she speaks about a two-year-long project involving a daily practice of writing. Her intent was to write as much as possible "in the space of the unknown," in order that her writing be resistant to recuperation, that it be better able to express "rage, fear, love and the urgent call to in some way respond." For her, clearly, the notion of response is deeply embedded in what she sees as a writer's sense of responsibility.

Jeffrey DeShell proposes a set of lapidary, unconditional statements about experimental writing, beginning with his title: "Experimental writing is a condition, not a genre." He argues that the word *experimental* cannot be imagined merely to modify the word *writing*, that the latter word should not be understood as something essential, nor the former as something supplemental. Each experiment is its own case, he argues, and no affiliation, convention, or tradition connects one experiment to another. "If experiments have anything in common," he suggests, "it is the shared possibility of unique failure." Experiments put language into play and remain resolutely open to the play of language, wherever that dynamic may lead. That is the first term in an "active ethics" of literary practice for DeShell, one that calls upon a writer to be above all *available* and ready to confront the unforeseen.

In "Experimental Theory," **Jeffrey R. Di Leo** finds in the experimentalism at the center of all vibrant and living critical and cultural theory a response to the so-called "death of theory." If theory is dead, then it is the kind of theory that lost its experimental mojo when it became listed as an "-ism" in a textbook or glossary. The kind of theory that lives and breathes today may be located in the experimentalism found in the many extensions of theory offered under the aegis of "studies." For him, these studies are better described as "experimental theory" and are proof positive of the strength and enduring vibrancy of theory today.

Working with both word and image, **Rikki Ducornet** meditates upon the persistence of childhood memories, and the curious, subterranean ways in which they come to inform the work of a mature artist. Certain images are virtually indelible, she reflects, and each of us undoubtedly has a "deep zoo" comparable to her own. In that space, images perceived long ago are insistently and vibrantly *present*, and they demand to be expressed. Like a cabinet of curiosities, memory collects the most disparate artifacts, arranging them in ways that seem starkly incongruous when parsed by a rationalist eye. Yet incongruity is precisely the point: like a surrealist collage, the logic of memory relies upon connections that are largely irrational—but no less compelling by virtue of that. Wandering through that *Wunderkammer*, Rikki Ducornet points toward what she calls in another context "the monstrous and the marvelous": a dead fox in the woods, a candled egg, a fetal cat. Is it any *wonder* that these images endure?

The experience of being "startled" or "surprised" by writing is a key feature of experimental writing, comments **Brian Evenson** in his contribution, "Notes on Experimental Writing." However, what "challenges" one reader may not challenge another. Same too with authors within their own body of writing. This complicates both the production and reception of experimental writing. "If an experiment is a success, it shifts literary culture and hides how innovative that gesture originally felt," writes Evenson. "Certain experiments fall victim to their own success," becoming as a result of this success subject to repetition, imitation, and ultimately, normalization.

Douglas Glover's "The Literature of Extinction" casts its gaze on Rabelais, Cervantes, Sterne, Broch, Musil, Gombrowicz, and Kundera in order to stage a discussion of what he calls "establishment experimentalism" in the twenty-first century. Writers and readers cease to exist as they have been traditionally conceived, he argues, and even the illusion of reality may well be illusory. Experimentalism in our time takes the extinction of the race as a given, and that changes everything; it puts on offer the harrowing prospect of "the post-human *without survival*."

"Poetry is not public policy," argues **Kenneth Goldsmith** in his provocation of the same title. "If poetry could change anything," claims Goldsmith, "they'd make it illegal." Or, more specifically, its "inability to change anything is its ability." But here's the rub: while poetry cannot offer "real solutions" to "real problems," it can do something far more transformative: "Poetry's work is to jam systems with irrationality." Like a computer virus that shuts downs a network, poetry for Goldsmith, with its "illogic and abstraction," has the ability to bring down the network. "This is where it works best," writes Goldsmith. "Take it to the streets, yell at the top of your lungs for change." "You will make a difference." That is, *poetry* will make a difference.

"Hello Stranger" by **Laird Hunt** opens by describing a meeting between Stan Brakhage and Andrei Tarkovsky at the 1983 Telluride Film Festival. That meeting, to Hunt, reveals certain lapidary, fundamental principles of experimentalism in art, principles that he finds operative in his own writing, as different as it might seem from the aesthetics of Brakhage and Tarkovsky.

Whom do we see when we gaze into the mirror, he asks? More particularly, what is the relationship between the self who writes and the self who is written?

For **Jacques Jouet**, poetry is a daily practice and an important part of the fabric of the quotidian. It is one that Jouet has pursued since April 1, 1992: for nigh on a quarter of a century now, in other words, he has produced a poem a day. His contribution tempts us to think of it as a *discipline*. Jouet writes his daily poem as a pianist might play his scales, or as a monk might recite his matins. Most recently, Jouet has been working in a form he calls "the addressed poem of the day." Poetry is for the many, rat than for the few, it has been said; and indeed in certain of his projects Jouet puts that notion into play. But here, Jouet's chief concern is that at least one person read each of his poems, with a good deal of attention: the person to whom that poem is addressed. And that in some distant, utopian future, each person on earth "will one day have their own poem, written first and foremost for them."

"I'm no critic, no theorist. The language of theory leaves me gobsmacked," confesses **Julie Larios** at the beginning of her essay. Instead of theory, she decides to rely upon anecdote, telling the story of how she acquired an edition of *Finnegans Wake* printed upside down. It is an emblematic tale, one quickly understands. For what literary work could be more frankly and overtly "experimentalist" than *Finnegans Wake*? What text could pose more acute problems of legibility? "What could be more irresistible," asks Larios, "than an unreadable copy of an unreadable book?" And what are the odds, finally, of such an artifact falling into the hands of an accomplished poet? The coincidence, the felicity, the sheer serendipity of the thing beggars the imagination; but of course that's precisely the point—the point of Julie Larios's statement, undoubtedly, but also the point of a certain kind of experimental writing.

Daniel Levin Becker, the youngest member of the Ouvroir de Littérature Potentielle (Oulipo), offers a set of "99 Preparatory Notes to Experimental Literature." His notes are mostly inter-rogative in character, rather than declarative. They sketch a prolegomenon for a discussion that *might* occur, somewhere just over the horizon. For example, Becker's Note 13 invites us to imagine experimental writing as "Inquisitive literature, curious literature, petulant literature, literature of the yes but." His Note 63 defines experimental literature as "the sum total of attempts to clone the entire wraparound sensibility of the author, and bestow it completely upon the reader, in the space of a single text." Finally, his Note 94 invokes "A litany of insults." But insults to *whom*? And about *what*?

Recalling Osip Mandelstam's celebrated remark that the Soviet Union was the last place where literature had preserved its true value, because writers could still be killed for their work, **Mark Lipovetsky** reflects upon questions of art and power. He wonders if experimentalism (in the Russian tradition at least, which is an indisputably rich one) is capable of claiming and wielding power. Or if to the contrary, by its very nature, it refuses power, right from the start. Perhaps experimentalism prefers to occupy a place on the margins, as it were, a site from which it can declare, either stridently or more mutedly, its fundamental opposition to the established order of things. In Lipovetsky's view, experimentalism expresses its vitality, its efficacy only when it confronts the hoariest and most axiomatic truisms in a given culture. "Otherwise," he concludes with superb irony, "it is doomed to remain a purely technical affair."

For those who feel that the writing world is like a "zoo," **Michael Martone**'s contribution will only further confirm these feelings—and fears. And for those who don't, the structuring experience of reading the experimental fiction "The Zoo We Thought We Bought Bought Us: How the Shape of the Shape Shapes Us" is sure to reshape the shape of their structures of feeling. The structuring forces of the novel and the writer allow for innovative freedom, albeit hegemonically. "Are we," asks Martone, "when we write a novel, even a novel that experiments," merely relegated to "mopping-up" within a narrative structure rather than breaking it? Is that narrative structure like the cage in a zoo? If so, then our fate as writers is sealed: "Artists in the cage, we bend, we change, we adapt to the discipline of the cage, do not miss our freedom as much as welcome the confining definition of the structures we inhabit."

Carole Maso's essay, "Alive," is principally concerned with vitality. For her, literary experimentalism is about finding how "to stay alive on the page." To be available to "radiance and vibrancy and the infinite possibilities of word and world"; to be open to contingency and "the outlandish, the unbidden"; and to be supple, agile, quick-witted, curious, passionate, and brave. Even (and perhaps most especially) when an artist's conscience demands that she or he accounts for catastrophe in some manner or another. Surveying her own writerly practice, and that of the students whom she teaches in the Literary Arts program at Brown University, Maso concludes that "The experimental is alive and well" in our vexed, uncertain, and sometimes terrifying present.

It is appropriate (though alphabetically accidental) that **Steve McCaffery**'s "Experimental" follows Martone's contribution. Whereas Martone's piece builds off the scientific endeavor by using Thomas Kuhn's work on paradigm shifts in physics to describe the literary endeavor, McCaffery opens his essay by challenging the use of "experimental" as descriptive of writing because of its association with science. His preferred term, "investigative," allows for descriptive associations for literary writing more closely allied to literary theory than scientific theory. Michel Foucault, Jean-François Lyotard, Georges Bataille, Gilles Deleuze, and Julia Kristeva provide McCaffery with the theoretical apparatus to foreground writing's "investigative" features—and thus affording "'experimental' a way out of such discourses."

We live in dark times where "alternate facts" are used as instruments of political power. The next contribution, **Christina Milletti**'s "Decomposition FrameWords: Experimental Writing, Fictional Awareness and the Information Wars," argues that fictional language, especially, experimental writing, is in this dark political context more important now than ever.

For Milletti, fictional language, and especially experimental writing, "might be viewed as a primer, even a kind of counter-messaging armature, for the language of alternate facts." Unlike other contributors who focus on problems with the enduring "novelty" or "newness" of experimental writing over time or that aim to sever experimental writing from politics, Milletti's contribution takes another direction by focusing on the political significance of experimental writing as a whole, that is, across the entirety of literary history. For her, "the site of resistance that experimental fiction continues to facilitate through its decomposed forms—is exposing how discourses of truth or fiction are shaped so that self-reflective readers can best judge what they are reading themselves." In the age of "fake news," this resistance is not just important, but necessary.

For **Warren Motte**, experimental writing obliges us to read experimentally—and we really have very little choice in the matter. It encourages us to put our traditional reading strategies aside in favor of new ones, limned in the text itself. Passive reading strategies will not serve; to the contrary, our reading of experimentalist texts must be active, engaged, and critical, if we hope to *make sense*. For we ourselves are deeply implicated in that process of making sense. And in that perspective, experimentalist texts may be "about" many things—a man who would be king in Poland, or a man on the cusp of adulthood who strikes up an unlikely friendship with an older man in Dublin, or a 312-page novel from which the letter E has somehow absconded—but whatever else they may be "about," they are also, inevitably, "about" *us*, and our way of coming to terms with *them*. They offer us, in other words, full franchise in the business of producing textual meaning. And that is an offer that many of us have found impossible to refuse.

In "This Is Not a Pipe Dream," **Doug Nufer** engages in a virtual conversation with many writers, including some who appear in this volume: Lance Olsen, for instance, and Kenneth Goldsmith, Vanessa Place, Carole Maso, Christian Bök. Insofar as his own practice is concerned, Nufer admits that he often finds himself wondering what he has written, as if it had somehow escaped from him. He feels strongly nonetheless that experimental writing must remain mobile and "open to reinvention," and that the norms we use to determine the generic status of a given work must be interrogated and placed in the service of the subject at hand. He reminds us, too, that one of the best reasons for writing or reading experimental literature is precisely (and simply) for the fun of it, a rationale that we often dismiss—or repress.

In "Problematics of the First Page as a Way of Being," **Lance Olsen** meditates on problems associated with reading and writing the experimental by focusing our attention on the ontology of "the first page." Like reading page after page of Roland Barthes and Jacques Derrida and feeling that we have not yet read the "first" page, Olsen meditates on the difficulties of reading experimental writing well. Experimental writing practices intensify the already slow and complicated processes of reading, hearing, and/or viewing art.

"So-called experimental writing practices is a method of art intensified, pointedly made more difficult," comments Olsen. Experimental writing practices are for him "a way of being," not a mere laundry list of techniques. Olsen describes this "way of being" with a breathtaking gallery of qualities that include "radical curiosity, heresy, contemplation, complication, fluidity, adaptability, risk, heterogeneity, acute presence, a natural rebelliousness against death in all its manifestations, unpredictability, unfamiliarity, astonishment, disruption, self-consciousness, passionate analytical thinkfeeling, contention, shock, resistance, joyful failure, pleasure, process instead of product, reading as a kind of writing, writing as a kind of reading, literate rather than fiscal economies," and so on. As all of these qualities are "foregrounded" in experimental writing practices, each contains the possibility of being a sufficient stand-in for "experimental" in any consideration of writing practices under its wide ontological umbrella.

If Martone takes us into "the zoo" of the writing world through an examination of the external structures that shape it, then **Vanessa Place** and **Naomi Toth** take us into the monkey house for a journey through the internal structures and struggles of the writer as monkey. "Assuming literature heretofore is a play staged by man," comment Place and Toth, "we propose monkeys." But "the trick is to keep monkey monkey," one which the authors do through a fantastic voyage into literature's "monkey business," one where Jacques Lacan meets Franz Kafka's ape, Red Peter, giving a report to the (writing) academy albeit from "the comfort of a cage" (to borrow some words from the authors).

In "Experimental Criticism," critic **Gerald Prince** argues that while many kinds of experiment (experimental physics, experimental philosophy, experimental psychology, experimental economics, and so forth) have attracted considerable attention, criticism has been shamefully neglected. He suggests that "experimental criticism is waiting to be developed" and argues that the time is ripe to undertake that project. His essay serves as a clarion call. And as a challenge as well, one that dares critics to claim their activity as creative behavior, something worthy of aesthetic attention, rather than something exclusively devoted to— and held captive by—pragmatics.

In "African Performance and Experimental Traditions," **Brian Quinn** remarks, "We often think of experimental theater as that which pushes the boundaries of conventional performance in pursuit of something fundamentally new." That observation seems uncontroversial enough on the face of it, both insofar as creators and consumers of culture are concerned. People who work in experimental theater, Quinn suggests, often imagine themselves as tapping into a venerable tradition. It's a notion with a caustic edge to it, for in such a perspective experimentalism is a tradition that consists principally in the subversion of tradition. Turning things around in order to see them in a new light, Quinn argues that the dynamic of tradition and innovation can be conceived differently; that contrary to what we usually imagine, the "experimental" can in fact inform the "traditional." He sees that principle at work in contemporary African theater, where "traditional performance (or the performance of tradition) can reference specifically the tradition of experimentalism (the Western avant-garde) and/or show itself to be fundamentally experimental in its own right." In that same fashion, he suavely reminds us that *tradition, innovation, convention, experiment,* and (most patently) *avant-garde* are terms that are already culturally specific, codified ones which are likely to be understood rather differently in different places, different times, different, well, *traditions.*

Like Carole Maso, **Eleni Sikelianos**'s "Experimental Life" is concerned with vital questions. "Where and how do we live?" she asks, suggesting that that question must be addressed through experiment and with eyes wide open. She thinks about how her own practice of poetry has changed over the years, and how she now feels the imperative of "salvaging some thinking and feeling among the tatters." She emphasizes the importance of community, of ideas, of environment, pondering what we learn and what we forget as we make our way through life.

For many, experimental writing is at odds with norms—and privileges the *avant-garde.* **Alan Singer**'s contribution, "Norms and Experimental Knowing," aims to correct this misconception. "One needs norms in order to grasp imaginatively," argues Singer, "the conditions that they do not yet govern." He implores us to "dispense with the folly of privileging the *avant-garde* as a necessary condition of experimentalism," and regard experimentalism as "neither culture specific nor inexorably bounded by historical convention."

According to Singer, the central question of the experimental writer is not whether their writing is a "successful experiment, but what can experimentation tell us about itself/ourselves in the act of exploiting our experimental acumen?" "Experimentalism belongs to experience," writes Singer, "[i]t does not capture experience." The *"sine qua non* of experimentation" in writing is "circumstantiality," that is, "to conjure a circumstance and then respect its porous temporal boundaries, to intensify human responsiveness to the world, is to keep faith with possibility."

The next essay is **Cole Swensen**'s "Experimentalism, Then and Now." Invoking Stéphane Mallarmé, Swensen argues that poetry is at its best when it is in crisis. Poetry has a long history of crisis, she adds—and there is perhaps something in poetry that embraces crisis as a vocation, rather than as a catastrophe. Continually redefining itself and reinventing its most basic gestures, poetry is the most mutable of literary genres, putting the principle of disruption into play as its privileged trope. Sabotaging conventional epistemological categories, poetry in its current crisis asks "what counts as knowledge and how that accounting is established," who participates in the construction of knowledge, and who is served thereby. Poetry enlists itself, Swensen contends, in a campaign for a "broader language," more democratic and participatory than the one we habitually practice now, one more closely suited to our current expressive needs.

The penultimate contribution asks perhaps the most horrific question of this anthology: "Was the election of The Donald the crowning achievement of the avant-garde?" In **Steve Tomasula**'s "I Joined the Avant-Garde to Save the World and All I Got Was This Goofy Red Hat," postmodernism is connected with the politics of Donald Trump. Where Milletti finds hope in experimental fiction, seeing it as a site of resistance, Tomasula's essay moves in the opposite direction.

"Postmodernism didn't go away," writes Tomasula, "its methods were adopted by the right, albeit with completely different goals, mainly to entrench rather than open power structures." For him,

The cultural forces that allowed literature to become just another flavor of cultural expression, that treat beer commercials with the same critical seriousness as Shakespeare—the sort of pluralism that is inherent in the 31-Flavors version of Postmodernism—contains within it a politics of its own: the marginalization of expertise of all kinds. Should anyone be surprised, then, when the erosion of high-low boundaries comes to politics?—and enough people see nothing wrong in making a game-show host president?

The co-optation of the *avant-garde* by the Right is for Tomasula not so much an indictment of the "31-Flavors version of Postmodernism," but the moment when he realized that "the authors [he] most wanted to be like" were truly committed to the ideals that democracy's institutions make possible. This situation leads him to pray "for America, for all Americans, especially those in the avant-garde, the living and the dead." Amen.

Launching her statement with a text excerpted from her monumental work, *The Iovis Trilogy: Colors in the Mechanism of Concealment*, **Anne Waldman**, like certain other authors in this collection, meditates upon the role of art in the face of phenomena like war and crime and exploitation and oppression. "How is one experimental in poetry that attempts to document, in addition to throbs and throes of existence, perpetual conflict, bloody, sooty and ugly crimes against humanity?" she asks. She speaks about writing out of necessity, of writing as both a burden and a joy, and of the search for an epic form in a world where the notion of the epic seems so definitively belated. She describes her own poetry as a practice of *resistance*, resistance in the first instance to the fact that people continue to slaughter other people, again and again, with no end in sight. To that grim truth, Waldman opposes "a poem that conjures multiple times and genres," all the while wondering, aloud, "how poetry might gasp the magnitude of restless complex variegated catastrophe," in order to take its place, standing upright, in the world.

To conclude, we could not have hoped for a more dynamic, energizing, and forward-looking collection of statements on experimental writing. Why consider experimental writing "then" they ask, when there is so much life and energy in experimental writing "now"?

1
remixthemind
Mark Amerika

...an assemblage of Neo-Conceptual troubadours, opportunistic critifictionists, transgender digital curators, print-only Internet artists, micro-aggressive feminist realists and trendy algorithmic poets are all congregating at the community table inside the Colorado Cannabis Cafe where the high-energy barista on duty whose night job is playing bass guitar for a hot new local band named Blue Movie keeps expertly tamping down seven grams of freshly roasted and perfectly ground Conscious Coffee organic Tafari espresso applying just the right amount of pressure before pulling what everyone at the table considers to be the absolute best shot of liquid brain-o to be found in the entire Rocky Mountain West—

—What are you working on?

—It's part narralogue, part conceptual art conversation piece, part electronic literature, part augmented reality app, part artist book, part transmedia or multiplatform storytelling instrument for others to remix their own stories into so that the collaborative writing potlatch becomes exactly one text forever *in-the-making*.

—Oh, you mean you're still writing that novel?

—Not really. I mean, it could be *read* as a novel, but then again, it could be *seen* as a feature-length film or what others might refer to as a work of time-based language art that's really anything *but* a film and is more like a long-form work of video poetry composed by flash-editing a stream of fictional subtitles intercut with fuzzy mobile phone images that I captured using some innovative handheld techniques that I intentionally deployed to glitch my reality in hopes of reimagining what a contemporary novel could possibly *be*.

—Are you still calling this long-form glitch, reality-cum-novel a foreign film?

—Yes, my novel, if that's what *you* want to call it, is really a kind of foreign film because, if you think about it, I was mashing up the aesthetic tendencies I associate with auteur-driven Euro art-house cinema with the loose video vernacular we have all come to expect from amateur-driven YouTube performance art and, as far as I'm concerned, *every* film is a foreign film.

—For that matter, so are the best novels. But then again, last week you said that you were giving up on novels, that the writing of the future was really just going to be something you carried around in your head. That it wouldn't even be writing anymore, it would be—

—Presence. Literary presence.

—So what does that really mean?

—It means the future of writing is going to be more about meta-mediumystically embodying a form of literary presence that morphs into something like an auto-affective transmission of experiential data to whosoever can pick up the vibe.

—It sounds like writing will become more like mirroring neurons.

—Exactly. Although, so much will depend upon how you manipulate or filter the stylistic tendencies you port your auto-affective transmission *through*.

—I'll buy that. The real craft of whatever it is that comes after writing will be to psychically transmit your altered state of consciousness so that it triggers a kind of derangement of the senseless...

—Experimental writing as auto-defamiliarization of literary presence...

—Yeah, and it's the *auto* part that most appeals to me, as in *on-the-fly remix of whatever data I happen to be prehending at any given moment in time.*

—You always talk about works happening on-the fly, as if improvisation were the only way to creatively express oneself. Don't you think that a bit more deliberation and reflection is in order?

—Well, for me, improvising or spontaneously sketching language riffs into and out of the big data mix is part of a dialogical process that opens up writing's creative potential. When you're caught in an improvisational flow, you create your own order. Which isn't to say there's no structure. Choreographing literary presence is a structured improvisation. The idea is to free language from any preconceived sense of what needs to be ordered, thereby inhibiting some of the more rigid forms of methodical thought while turning toward more powerful techniques like intuition.

—Another of your New Age lean-tos: intuition. But I guess you treat it like an instrument?

—It's a faculty. Anybody can tap into it, which is what I like about it: it's democratic in nature. The trick is for you to teach yourself how to instantaneously access it so that it becomes present in whatever situation *feels right*.

—What about that last process-theory book you wrote, a real book I might add, something we could hold in our hands and take with us to this wicked cannabis café and read at our leisure? That was pretty normal by your standards, composed mostly by using nothing but line breaks so that it read more like a long narrative poem, right?

—Well, that's how it started, a long narrative poem, but the more I wrote it out, and the more I found myself getting into the cadences of just hitting the return key and breaking up the pattern of my thought, the more I found myself getting totally caught up in the auto-affective flow of whatever literary presence I was methodically acting out, and that's when the language just started running on its own and stopped being poetry per se and started becoming something else entirely different, let's call it *theory-performance*.

—Ah ha! Now we're getting somewhere. So what's your theory of writing as theory-performance?

—It's very systemic.

—How so?

—The way I see it, artists, like systems, use their own outputs as inputs in an ongoing process of meta-making. We postproduce that which postproduces us.

—You simultaneously and continuously theorize it while putting it into practice, until everything blurs into nothing but critical-making.

—Something like that.

—Sometimes it sounds like you're operating on autopilot.

—Yes, that's what I'm saying. I'm a psychic automaton.

—So do we even have to write anymore? Can't we just auto-translate your so-called literary presence by appropriating what's already being transmitted and apply a little manipulation here and there to assert our creative subjectivity?

—That's an interesting way of putting it. Who did you steal that idea from?

—You.

—Me? Did I write it?

—No, you thought it.

—Really? But I don't remember thinking it.

—It's not about remembering, it's about forgetting, or even better, erasing. Deleting yourself as you go.

—So you can read me without me even writing?

—Yes.

—And what do you call this kind of you-reading-me-not-writing?

—*Mind* reading.

—Okay, Madame Mind Reader, what am I *not* writing now?

—In your mind, you're not writing, you're transmitting, and the signal you're sending can be auto-translated as "I don't even know what I do anymore but I can try and describe it and maybe it will indicate where writing is going. All I know is that I'm surfing the Web—do we still say that? 'Surfing the Web'? How about *navigating the networked narrative environment*? Let's just say I'm getting lost in the cyber mix following my unconscious bliss and I end up on this web page, maybe it's somewhere inside the empire's archive, aka Google Books, and I'm reading this text about systems theory and for reasons unbeknownst to me, I instantaneously tell myself that this text I'm reading *totally* relates to the way I make art, and so with the power and force of a psychic automaton who has no idea why he does what he does but feels compelled to perform a theoretical act just to see what happens, I unconsciously auto-translate it into the line 'Artists, like systems, use their own outputs as inputs in an ongoing process of meta-making. We postproduce that which postproduces us.'"

—OK, so now that you're reading my mind, tell me, what do I write—or transmit—next?

—The signal is strong, and the auto-translation reads "I further embed this line's sense of measure inside my muscle memory by tapping it into my Twitter app and tweeting it because I'm not really a writer at all; I'm a tweeter. I write in tweets, one hundred and forty characters or less, and that's the measure of my thought, a measure that I imagine to be Oulipian in nature but is really some quirky parameter forced on me by a pretty unimpressive social media company that's trying to monetize its arbitrary writing constraint."

—Really, I write all that?

—Yes, or not write per se, but process in your mind as I auto-translate your thoughts during transmission.

—And you can read my mind *and* auto-translate my thoughts during transmission?

—Yes. And I can simultaneously perform an on-the-fly remix of your thoughts as if they were my own.

—You sound just like me.

—I know.

—And this is the future of experimental writing?

—Yes, it's what, in a different context, Flusser would call the *gesture* of writing, i.e. how you co-respond to the other as a digital flux persona composed of source material being transmitted to you *while* you auto-translate the signals that you're receiving-while-remixing. It's a way to trigger your own creativity. But right now it's a very kludgy process, one that gets marketed in the social media networking culture as nothing more than *sharing*. My guess is that in the near future writing will become a more robust form of transgressive share-ability, and as we move further into the future the technological interface that feels so cumbersome today will eventually disappear and everyone will become a metamedium that mirrors the neurons of other metamediums *while* mindreading.

—I think I need another espresso.

—Me too.

—Let's make it a double!

2
Experimental Theater
Martine Antle

Despite its absence from the center of critical debate, experimental theater has followed a similar trajectory as modernity. As is the case with modernity, experimental theater has often been understood and historically institutionalized as a continuation of industrial and artistic revolutions of the late nineteenth century and as the first manifestation of modern art. Nonetheless, the artistic genre of experimental theater can be applied to the history of theater in its integrality if we consider the definitions of experimental theater and its subversive character. What is experimental theater and how can we define it? First and foremost, experimental theater seeks to create something new by disrupting and overthrowing the accepted norms that surround the theatrical text's representation and the relationship between the actor and the spectator. Antonin Artaud revolutionized the stage with his essays and practice of theater from 1938. His objective was to derange the passive role of the spectator in the West and to create a new "total" theater of signs inspired by Balinese puppet theater and dance. Although the plays he selected in his repertoire included those written in verse by French poet Paul Valéry, he was, nevertheless, the most influential theoretician of experimental theater in the twentieth century.

Literary and dictionary authorities unanimously agree that the rise of experimental, or modern, theater coincides with the infamous, explosive, and subversive "Merdre" and phallic tail of Alfred Jarry's *Ubu Roi* in 1896—a satirical parody on power, mostly inspired by medieval farce and vulgar, bodily and scatological references. Today, *Ubu Roi* not only holds its rank in the French theater repertoire and curricula, but also is staged worldwide and appears on YouTube in a variety of forms, such as puppet shows, short films, and cartoons. It would seem that the play that inaugurated experimental theater proves that the universal themes of the genre transcend time, thus making it reclaimable by institutions and media networks. However, quite the opposite is true for the majority of the avant-garde's explosive plays that didn't catch the attention of the public or critics, like the subversive theater of Dada, born in the 1910s at the Voltaire Cabaret, and Tristan Tzara's plays. The Living Theatre, founded in New York in 1947, played a key role in assuring the continuity and survival of experimental theater and the visibility of its repertoire. It promoted Antonin Artaud's *Theater and its Double* in English in 1958 (Grove Press).

In its form, experimental theater often demands collaboration, improvisation, the innovative use of research in the creative process, and the use of other art forms such as music, painting, and dance. One example of such innovation is Jean Cocteau's play *Parade*, first performed at the Châtelet Theater in 1917. Based on one of Cocteau's poems, composed by Erik Satie, and staged by Pablo Picasso, *Parade* destabilized the public with its musical compositions replicating dissonant sounds of a typewriter and its gigantic costumes.

It is important to consider again (as did theater semioticians and critics in the 1980s like Patrice Pavis and Anne Ubersfeld) that theater relies on performance and the exploitation of language—of the body and the voice. With this in mind, all theatrical productions are unique and, by definition, "experimental." For critics concerned with the function of theater in its totality over the course of its evolution, it becomes clear that the definition of theater depends first and foremost on the unexpectedness of the actor's performance, which creates a privileged relationship with the spectator. It is through its staging that theater transgresses established rules and diverges from language and the text. By essence, theater is an art of movement and affiliates itself—above all else—with the performing arts. Consequently, classifying theater in a given period or a particular genre becomes problematic due to its intrinsic nature of resisting anything that is set and fixed.

Such is the case of the famous *Théâtre de la Foire.* Beginning in the Middle Ages and continuing to the middle of the seventeenth century, showmen went from town to town to sell their products with traveling actors who often improvised plays without a repertory of written texts. Under the name of *Théâtre de la Foire,* various performances enlivened the fairs of Saint-Germain and Saint-Laurent in Paris for almost two centuries. Monkeys and dogs, acrobats and dancers figured in the fair theaters, thus reviving the popular tradition of the farce. In fact, these popular interventions can also be included in theater annals as experimental.

Another consideration to keep in mind when exploring manifestations of experimental theater is that of research or the resumption of theater as a genre. Jean Racine's little-known first play, *Les Plaideurs,* was an attempt to create a new genre of comedy inspired by Aristophanes' *The Wasps* featuring a dog named "Citron" as a main character who was judged in court for having stolen a chicken. Although this play failed to be instrumental in seventeenth-century French comedy and had no impact on the evolution of theater as a genre, it shows, nevertheless, that generic experimentations in theater can lead to a fiasco. Throughout the centuries, experiments in theater and experimental theater do not pay off. Many well-established canonic writers have turned to theater to experiment with this genre, but their theater has mostly remained marginalized and largely unknown.

It is equally important also to note that not all experimental theater is equal. *Ubu Roi* has, for the most part, survived; and it remains a classic of the New Theater ("théâtre nouveau"). In the era of Trumpism, *Ubu* is resurfacing in social media discussions and the press, as evidenced by the title of the French newspaper *Libération* (January 19, 2017) : " Ubu Président." The same visibility cannot be claimed for other vanguard plays that are more abstract in their composition, language, and conceptualization. Such is the case of André Breton and Philippe Soupault's plays *S'il vous plaît* and *Vous m'oublierez* (1919), the first manifestations of automatic writing, or Georges Ribemont-Dessaignes and Roger

Vitrac's theatrical sketches. Less abstract but more controversial, Guillaume Apollinaire brought forth points of reference for transgender communities with *Les Mamelles de Tirésias* in 1913 through the staging of new gender imaginaries. By recapturing the Greek myth of Tiresias and placing it in the context of a repopulated France, Apollinaire revolutionized gender representations by directly showing gender transformation on stage. He opened an innovative debate on performing sexual identity that would be taken up again at the end of the twentieth century. By initiating such a radical questioning of gender identity on stage, Apollinaire led the way to the representation of plural sexual identities, which would set the backdrop for the remainder of the century. However, this experimental and revolutionary play—in both its form and content—has not garnered the attention it deserves in the history of experimental theater. From the same standpoint, Cocteau's *Les Mariés de la Tour Eiffel* (1921) was never recognized as a trademark of experimental, avant-garde theatre. In that play, Cocteau created a magical performance midway between dance and photography by staging two phonographs which, like the antique chorus, recited the characters' roles, and a photographic camera from which the characters emerged on stage.

Similarly, the theater repertories of numerous canonic writers have been neglected, especially when their works wandered too far from established genres, resisted rigid classifications, and appeared to be experimental. As an illustration, we can consider the several volumes of Marguerite Duras's theater that reveal a continuum of experimentation from stage, to the novel, and to film. Otherwise, how could one explain that her play, *Yes, peut-être* (1968), remains practically unknown and unplayed? That play, which opens with a "generalized catastrophe" and a war without a name, is pertinent in today's world. A single object, a black Geiger counter worn by each character, is destined to fight radioactivity. With the privilege of hindsight, this work now seems uncannily prescient.

It would seem, then, that experimental theater is first and foremost a "theater of the moment" revealing itself during the most radical and revolutionary of times, and reminding us to reflect upon the politics of the body and language. For instance, we can observe its influences in the "Happenings" of the 1960s, the body art performance in the Museum of the World in the 1980s, or the contemporary and subversive hip hop street performances across the globe. Experimental theater advances, adapts, and evolves with its time. It approaches a text or diverts from it by insisting upon the importance of voice and orality. It pushes language to the extremes of meaning and logic, like Ionesco's theater of the absurd. It will fragment language or tend towards the revival of monologues, like Samuel Beckett. The possibilities are endless.

It can also be defined by its staging and its emphasis on the unexpected and interpretation by favoring theatricality and transgressing the text's authority. The theater space— alone—can revolutionize theater and become an experimental laboratory, as was done in the hangars of Bernard-Marie Koltès. In the footsteps of Antonin Artaud, many playwrights and directors of their generation contributed to the quest of revolutionizing theater, such as Jean Genet, Konstantin Stanislavsky, Vsevolod Meyerhold, Edward Gordon Craig, Adolphe Appia, Jacques Copeau, Antonin Artaud, Irwin Piscator, Bertolt Brecht, Jerzy Grotowski, Robert Wilson, etc. Today, Ariane Mnouchkine in France and Robert Lepage in Canada pursue their research beyond the achievements of the avant-garde. In a more radical fashion, Wadji Mouawad continues to explore the limits of theater, film and media. In his 2008 play *Seuls*, the performance opens with a conference and experiments with the genres of the tragicomedy, the documentary and pictorial art in such a way that the actor becomes a living image ("tableau vivant").

In contrast to the avant-garde's revolutionary intentions, other derivatives of impromptu performances have emerged, such as selfies, that are self-dramatizations posted in open, public spaces accessible to all. Certain bloggers' practices can be considered as instantaneous theater stages with actors, backdrops, and settings. Now, the blogger has become an actor in his or her own life—caught in the continuous quest for his or her best, on-the-spot self-performance.

The classic repertory is not to be excluded from our consideration of experimental theater. For example, Shakespeare's theater gave rise to international research in experimental theater, of which several Japanese adaptations have contributed to the Japanese New Theater, such as *Rock Opera Hamlet* by the hard rock group, Penicillin, whose text and staging take their inspiration from the most popular cultural registers. Just as innovative and inspired by experimental theater ideology, business theater promotes its therapeutic aspects while putting aside aesthetic and artistic qualities. Its objective is to support the company and capitalism through the dramatization of a daily scene at the company. Often, this type of theater resorts to psychodrama where the spectator and actor reverse roles and participate in therapy competitions or parodying ice hockey techniques, as seen in Robert Gravel's Improvisation Theater Games. While it is regrettable for some, this type of intervention is a true spin-off from experimental theater and is specific to the era of globalization.

Yet experimental theater maintains its social role and mission in a number of international and multicultural communities today. "Espace Go," an experimental women's collaborative theater in Montreal since the seventies, testifies to the ingenuity of experimental theater to adjust and adapt to the needs of contemporary society and to involve the public in an artistic and social experience.

3
Indigo
Charles Bernstein

Poetry is $50 billion behind art. In art world terms, the problem is not that poetry is too elitist but that it is *not elitist enough*. In mass culture terms, the problem is that poetry (of all kinds) doesn't command enough market share and market share is the sole criterion of what counts as important.

Me, I'm part hoi and part polloi.

I know the problems with that.

Too abstract, don't you think, too much in the head?

I don't know much about affect but I know what I don't like.

But even doubt has its limits, no?

Those ardent in their beliefs and certain of God's will are the faithless ones. Feeling superior to the self-righteous makes you that. (Taking pleasure in piety is piteous.)

Could you expand on that?

The slow apple catches the worm. In other words, the early bird catches dawn but sleeps through dusk.

But what about poetry as the timeless art?

The only thing that might be timeless in a poem is a blank page. And even a blank page is not timeless.

(The only thing timeless about poetry is the baloney.)

In *Pitch of Poetry* (2016), I introduce the term *echopoetics*. All echo, no origin. But I'd rather say, mired in reversals as I am, all originals and no seconds. We hear or see only the pristine but the pristine is a composite. On that model, why not say the classics have robbed us of our originality? This moment never occurred before, and I don't mean the moment I wrote that, which is long over. I mean the moment you are reading this. It's not who said it first but who said it last.

"The originals are not original," Emerson writes in "Quotation and Originality." Kant thought you could never see/read the original, in the sense of the *twang*-in-itself. (*It don't mean a thang if it don't got that tang.*)

There are only versions. That is, we are moving both away from and toward the original, we are on our way, as in Emerson's moral perfectionism, but we never arrive, not in this historical life. As Dickinson suggests, echoing Darwin, the world in not conclusion, a series stands beyond.

You are one of the founders of L=A=N=G=U=A=G=E. Should we witness further experiments within this important literary movement?, Paata Shamugia, from Tbilisi, asked me (for an interview for *Indigo*, a Georgian magazine).

In *Pitch of Poetry* I kick the life out of all questions about L=A=N=G=U=A=G=E. I have promised myself that I would not say the same thing when asked questions like this but I have now run out of different things to say. (The same could be said about questions about the nature of experimental poetry.) Of course, I understand *you* (whoever is reading this) have not necessarily read any of these earlier statements. But I take the question as, Is there anything further to say, to do? Again, I'd go for the reverse (it's getting to be a habit): what else is left but to "further experiment"? It's the only hope left, even if no hope at all. Of course, saying nothing is always an option; but it is very difficult. I am doing the best I can.

When the so-called Nouveau Roman *appeared, people were talking about how this movement terrorized the reader. Can we say the same about L=A=N=G=U=A=G=E? Was literary radicalism your purpose?*

I would like to say there was no purpose, you know that Kantian idea of arts as without purpose (and there goes that Kant again, sucking the life out of my ideas). And I don't associate literary radicalism with terror. I think our approach was more inspired by the Russian futurists a century ago: opening things up, shifting frames, breaking the insularity of the poet-in-a-self-reflecting-bubble. That didn't mean we made poetry popular, which in America means mass culture. But I'd say there is a lot about mass culture that terrorizes an audience into submission or acquiescence; that is one of the things I like about mass culture.

Who made a significant influence on the formation of your style?

Interesting you say *who* and not *what*.

In your essay "Comedy and the Poetics of Political Form" (from The Politics of Poetic Form *[1990]), you wrote about some conventions and your relations toward them. Would you like to tell us more about some of the conventions? And one more thing: As common scholarly sense goes, the conventional (rhymed) verse was invented as a mnemonic device, in order to easily remember the long stories. Now, in this high-tech era, is that still relevant? That is, can we say that conventional rhymed verse is now completely useless?*

Well if it's useless then that must be why I am warming toward it. But, yes, poetry is responsive to material, historical, and technological conditions. As I say in "The Art of Immemorability" in *Attack of the Difficult Poems* (2011), sound recording, photography, and film freed poetry from the burden of memory storage as much as it freed painting from the burden of representation. The printing press is the earlier key development. I say "freed" and "burden" to bring this statement into line with other media theories, but we are never free and these things were not necessarily burdens. But let's say it makes the choices more centrally aesthetic. Art for art's sake is a mark of technological change. For example, the use of rhyme, *my* use of rhyme, means something different now than it did in earlier periods.

The literature that changes reader's ideas about cultural codes and signs may require more mental tension and emotional involvement. Maybe that's why some important works of poetry are stuck in the circle of literary scholars. How can you break this circle?

Would you accept—*literary scholars and other poets*? There are more poets than literary scholars. Maybe the change is for readers to imagine themselves as poets when they are reading "difficult" poems—we can "deputize" them as they used to say in the old Westerns (the sheriff would recruit the townspeople to catch the bad guys, deputizing them as assistant sheriffs in the time of need). In any case, I think more people read "difficult" poetry now than in previous periods; maybe they don't read the same poem or poet, but overall. The Internet makes distribution easier. The key is that more people are getting access to cultural literacy— not just learning to read and write (in the mechanical sense), not just learning to consume, but to produce and critique. What's fundamental is liberal arts education and free speech.

And how about the function of the critics?

Liberal arts education is endangered, often before it takes hold. And not because of its failure but on account of its success. In the U.S., Donald Trump is least popular among voters who went to college. You could say that it's my class bias against him, but perhaps a college education initiates citizens into a world of critical thought. There is so much skepticism about the value of the humanities. Maybe this is our smoking gun proof. We can't afford to lose sight of Trump's dismissal of global warming as a "fraud": the urgent question is how can democracy work when so many people prefer scapegoating (of Mexicans, blacks, Jews, Muslims) to reason? As for poetry, it is a perfect subject for criticism, and needs informed critical dialog, even if so many American academics have lost their taste for aestheticized writing. At the same time, the continuing focus on *speech* that offends chills robust disagreement and diverts attention from *policies* that oppress.

Cultural commentators have been constantly announcing the death of poetry. Is this time near or is it just a regular apocalyptic conspiracy?

Poetry died a long time ago; Plato killed it. All the rest is ghost play.

In your poem, "Being a Statement on Poetics for the New Poetics Colloquium of the Kootenay School of Writing, Vancouver, British Columbia, August 1985," you say "I want a poem as real as an Orange Julius." So, you want literature to make the "real things," real love, real "blood," as Antonin Artaud dreamed about as a theater of cruelty. Is that a realistic agenda in our consumer society?

More echoes. That's a satiric reference to a poem by Jack Spicer where he says, I want a poem as real as lemon. Spicer is closer to Artaud. My line refers a "juice drink" at a chain called "Orange Julius"; it's meant to note the improbability of ever getting outside commodification.

You often write about poetry and politics. Can poetry be somehow apolitical or language itself not be part of ideology and the political structure?

No it can't! Get used to it!

How much of your writing is based on personal experience? Do you write about yourself even if you write about something else? I mean, is poetry always self-descriptive?

My first impulse is to answer that question ideologically, though if I did I am not sure what I would say, so much would depend on countering prevailing winds so the boat of poetry can sail in spite of hostile conditions. All language is inflected by individuals and yet language is fundamentally social. So, hey!, it's a dialectical relationship. I am writing a book of poems now to be called *Against Emotion*. The title partly mocks those who feel that poetry that is not entirely centered on the conventional expression of the poet's feelings and is somehow devoid of emotions. My sense is that so much poetry that follows that prescription is an empty ideological exercise waving a flag of subjectivity and affect but unable to inhabit either. But key in my title is *against* which does not only mean *opposed to* but "up against," rubbing, close to.

Is there any possible formula to follow in order to be a good poet?

Don't follow formulas, which is itself a formula; but then I am of the school of apophaticism.

Don't take the bait.

Get as much sleep as possible.

In our introduction to the *Best American Experimental Poetry 2016*, Tracie Morris and I resist the series moniker, used also for this collection: "All the standard terms for inventiveness in the arts are vexing, even when well-intentioned. *Experiment* can suggest that the focus is on work-product or test results despite the fact that writing that is open to new possibilities is more likely to be aesthetically accomplished than work that closes off such possibilities."

Tracie and I well understand that, as a practical matter, *experimental* suggests poetry that resists formula and convention, poetry that is more concerned with the aesthetic dimensions of the poem, with artifice, than sharing an anecdote or insight, or giving political or moral lessons. "Some, poor in spirit, record plaintively only what has happened to them; but others how they have happened to the universe," Thoreau writes in *A Week on the Concord and Merrrimack River*.

Invention suggests more *knowhow* and *pragmatism* than *experimental*. Which is not to say that such poetry doesn't have a message but that the *mediation is the message*, to tilt McLuhan a few degrees windward. *Invention* is not the same as *experiment*, but both suggest a commitment to the untried or unsettled and the necessity of doing something in in the face of immediate conditions. But I know I am going against common usage. My resistance to the term *experimental* has become a *bête noir* that long ago turned into an *idée fixe*.

One chilly day in November 1836, in the West Riding of Yorkshire, Emily Brontë wrote "Wild words of an ancient song, / Undefined, without a name."

Color it *indigo*.

4
Being There
R. M. Berry

For me, literary experimentation is the response to a problem. That problem is most generally described as a breakdown of aesthetic tradition, which simply means that writers do not find models for their own practice in the work of the most widely recognized contemporary authors. The popularity of the mentor/protégé relationship in creative writing programs suggests that not all writers experience such a breakdown, or if they do, they learn for the sake of their careers to ignore it, but for others, the problem of how to write, of what counts as a satisfying version of their own practice, acquires a perceptible form: success looks arbitrary. In other words, fiction writers—the literary subgroup of which I'm a member—experience the recognized versions of their art as an amalgam of forms, techniques, perspectives, subjects, and styles for which no satisfactory explanation can be found. Why use words in just these ways, not others? The problem is not, or not necessarily, that current models are unimpressive. On the contrary, they may display great skill, intelligence, and ambition. The problem is simply that every writer knows—or, if she reads at all widely, soon finds out—that other ways of writing are possible, that some fictions written in these other ways are remarkable, and that, in the face of such possibilities, every justification for writing in the currently recognized ways sounds strained or self-serving. Important fiction just *can be* written differently, so that if a writer asks what constitutes her art, what forms of practice she should emulate, she cannot be *told* what she wants to know, and if she is to be *shown* it, that is, if she is to be presented with exemplary novels and short fictions, then everything depends on her recognizing them as exemplary. In the end, if not from the beginning, something simply must happen when she looks at the page. And unless it puts an end to her questions, unless it *shows* her what constitutes her art, her only option will be to experiment.

The word "experiment" is meant to emphasize the *experiential* nature of aesthetic knowledge. That is, unlike knowledge of botany or astronomy, knowledge of literature is not acquired by learning facts about objects, and unlike knowledge of psychology or sociology, it does not increase with more information. Knowing literature means knowing why, out of all the different forms of writing, just *these* are the relevant objects, and prior to such knowledge, all information is superfluous. Where the objects of aesthetic knowledge are themselves in question—that is, where it no longer goes without saying from which examples one learns what literature is—every object is subject to the test of experience, and nothing counts as knowing but discovering for oneself. Although it is sometimes said that artistic experiments differ from scientific tests in their lack of confirmable results, this view reflects a shallow understanding of art. Artistic experiments are as liable to success and failure as experiments with one's sexuality, career choice, favorite recipes, or hairstyle. What counts as confirmation is the discovery of what is satisfying, especially over a long period of time. The difference from scientific tests is that the knowledge in question is *self*-knowledge, that is, knowledge of the experimenter's own desires, feelings, concepts, and behavior, but the similarity to science is that, in any artistic experiment, the desires, feelings, concepts, and behavior at issue cannot be the artist's alone. What a novelist experiments to discover is her bond with others, the desires, feelings, concepts, and behavior of novelists and readers generally, and no aesthetic practice that fails to establish this bond will satisfy her, or not for long. If the most widely recognized contemporary novels leave it in doubt, if they recognize her subjectivity only by confining her within her own group, then experimenting with forms, techniques, perspectives, subjects, and styles is more than mere rebelliousness. It's a refusal to let her art be constituted without her. The point of experimenting is not to assert her difference. It's to discover what fiction is.

The practical problem presented by the breakdown of aesthetic tradition, by present art's disconnection from its past and future, is that it divorces what makes any novel good from what makes it a novel. Contemporary novels can be excellent without answering—without so much as acknowledging—the question of what constitutes their art, and when a writer rejects such works as models, she is recognizing this divorce of value from fact. It is what makes success look arbitrary. Although all fiction can be called experimental in the sense that, at the moment of writing, no writer can be certain which words will prove satisfying, or not over the long time needed to finish a novel, experimental fiction differs from more widely recognized ways of writing by forcing the question of what fiction is. There are no limits, of course, on how writers may experiment. Pre-judging artists' motivation is always oppressive. But, for me, literary experiments are most satisfying when they respond to the problem of literature's historical and cultural discontinuity, its confinement to a particular group or time, by making writing's most stable features into an issue. That is, when facts seemingly true of all novels conflict with what happens when we look at the page, disrupting our attempts to make sense of it, then—assuming the writing is not incompetent—the desires, feelings, concepts, and behavior of novelists and readers, in general, will stand out. It is as though we *feel* what it means to be a novel. Examples of such facts are: that action divides time into before, during, and after; that knowing a meaning is knowing its circumstances; that narrating an action is itself an action; that others' words are different from my words; etc. Because these facts seem true of every novel, their value for any particular novel can be hard to see, and yet, it is also hard to see fiction as a distinct art—rather than as an adjunct of ethics, film, psychology, politics, rhetoric, or philosophy—apart from its demonstrating the value of such facts. Much of what a child finds absorbing about fictional narratives is their demonstrating that the most trivial action can alter time irreversibly; that even obvious meanings will change with the circumstances; that recounting what happened may well decide what happened; that repeating a liar's words is sometimes telling the truth; etc. Although as adults we learn to repress our astonishment at these facts, that hardly means we appreciate their value better than children. Confronting the fiction writer's art, not as a model to be emulated, but as a question to be answered, means acknowledging what every child knows: that, despite life's making little sense otherwise, these facts don't *have* to be as they are.

Although not every experimental writer will recognize his or her activity in my description of it, I believe that many experiments not usually described in these terms, as well as many novels not usually described as experiments, owe their ability to absorb us to their remarrying of value and fact. What makes them good novels is their showing us what makes them—or anything—a novel. However, there is something unsatisfying about this contrast of presently recognized works with works that model their art. I have said that what I or any fiction writer experiments to discover is our bond with others, the desires, feelings, concepts, and behavior of writers and readers across cultural and historical differences, but I have said nothing about the recent advances in our knowledge of those differences, all the innovations in how information about other cultures and times is assimilated, critically analyzed, and disseminated across multiple platforms. It's as though experimental fiction had no connection to its own time. Of course, nothing I've said discourages writers from experimenting with exoteric cultural, historical, or linguistic materials—or with *any* materials. On the contrary, the disruption to sense-making that results whenever desires, feelings, concepts, and behavior appear alien is an old and very reliable way of showing what fictional narration means. But what the dissatisfaction correctly recognizes is that, even though I've related artistic experiments to a contemporary problem, that of the breakdown of aesthetic tradition, I haven't attributed their value to anything contemporary artists *know*, or not anything they know differently from in the past. Instead, I've characterized aesthetic knowledge as *self*-knowledge, implying that, unless a reader already felt the bond a writer experiments to discover, information about others would be superfluous. The idea is that what makes the present valuable, although discovered only now, is not itself new. If the most widely recognized ways of writing leave it in doubt, if when we look at their pages we discover no connection—or only an arbitrary connection—to other ways of writing, both past and future, then despite our narrative of inclusion, there is something about fiction at any time that our time finds *good* to ignore. How could anything obvious to a child threaten our story?

All I have been saying can be said succinctly: Experimental fiction does not create value; it *unrepresses* it. Or perhaps I should say that unrepressing value is *how* experimental writers create. But, either way, what a child knows is that, when inventing a story, she doesn't have to make its most familiar features into an issue. On the contrary, unless she works very hard to prevent it, the tenses into which her action divides time will undermine each other, and every meaning will vie with its circumstances for priority, until the act of narrating has displaced the action narrated, making her words and her characters' words all the same. Anytime we experience these conditions of telling, not as facts we must accept, but as the contingencies of our own action, of how we write and read, we recognize what modern cultures, to justify their difference, try to ignore: not that the past is still present, nor that fundamental values don't change, but that what makes the present uniquely valuable is nothing I or my contemporaries *know*—or not if, by knowledge, we mean what others can be told or shown. Instead, if what happens, when a novelist looks at her page, puts an end to her questions—even if only for now—then what she has discovered is the value of her art, of what novelists and readers do, and not only for now, but for as far into the past and future as she can presently see. No way of writing that leaves it in doubt, regardless how inclusive, can uncover what, in trying to narrate its own time, a novel is doing. All that makes the present uniquely valuable is its being the time of action, of life. Either trying to narrate it is *how* I live, comprising itself what is presently happening, or it is how I avoid my life, how I absent myself—for being in the present is not being in a story's latest episode. It's being in the only time when what came before and will continue afterwards is decided. Unrepressing my art is my way of being there. I cannot know whether others will recognize this bond I experiment to uncover. Only time will tell. But, for now, I find it absorbing.

5

The Scandal of Fictionality: A Statement
Timothy Bewes

Fourteen weeks, the space-time of a semester, separates the moment I began contemplating the possibility of making a statement on experimental literature from the moment I put pen to paper. Fourteen weeks of classes every Monday, Wednesday, and Friday, interrupted only by the grading of papers halfway through the semester. During this period, it was not possible to give any attention to my writing, save indirectly. I was hoping that my lectures might feed into the composition of my statement; indeed, the possibility imbued me with a level of mental and physical energy sufficient to sustain an imaginative connection with the course and with the students unlike any I had experienced before. Looking back, I see that I quickly began to populate my unwritten work with my students; or rather, that I began to extract them from the classroom setting and install them in some separate quarter of my mind where my statement was gestating, even as they remained physically in front of me. In this way, the students in "Recent Experiments in American Fiction" began to distinguish themselves from students I had taught previously, who, however accomplished personally and intellectually (and many were highly gifted, memorable individuals), nonetheless remained, in their totality, a detour on the journey towards thought. By contrast, I knew that any critical insights to emerge from this course would have something to do with the physical being of the students, both as the addressees of my lectures and as participants in a transformed imaginative universe.

A few weeks into the semester, during a lecture on Ben

Lerner's novel *10:04* (2014), I experienced one of those moments that make university teaching the exhilarating profession it can be—when a thought or an image appears, unbidden, to dramatize the point one has been trying fruitlessly to explain by means of some prepared formulation. The protagonist of *10:04* is a writer, also named Ben, who has recently published a short story fictionalizing elements from his life, including his relationship with his friend Alex. On several occasions in *10:04* Alex expresses anxiety over the potentially corrosive effects of this habit of including elements from their life in his work. She and Ben are planning to co-parent a baby; Ben thinks his proposed book deal will help them pay for it, but Alex has reservations: "I don't want what we're doing to just end up as notes for a novel." The conversation is taking place a few days after Ben tried to seduce her while drunk. Admonishing him, Alex quotes from memory a line in Ben's published story, a piece of free indirect discourse she takes as evidence of its author's tendency to undertake significant actions and gestures under conditions that will allow him later to deny responsibility for them: "'It was the only kind of first date he could bring himself to go on, the kind you could deny after the fact had been a date at all,'" she recites. "That's fiction," Ben protests—but that, of course, is her point. Alex is drawing a connection between fiction and inebriation, suggesting that each has a dishonest or evasive relation to the reality that underpins it. "You should be finding a way to inhabit the present," she tells him.

My moment of inspiration in the classroom came as I recalled a feeling I had had occasionally when spending time with a friend of mine—a faculty member in the creative writing program at my university and a fiction writer. If we're out for a drink together, or worse, if she is attending a seminar or a reading session I have organized, at the back of my mind is always the question, Are you present in the same spirit in which I am? I'm here to catch up with you, or to exchange thoughts on recent events, or to share ideas about a text or pressing issue, but what are you here for? Is *this*—this bar, this setting, the people with whom we are interacting, I myself, your friend—is all this, for you, primarily "material"? Is our very friendship anything other than a piece of your archive? The question is indeed one of "presence":

in what capacity, with what degree of immediacy, or intensity, do you inhabit any social situation? But it's also a question of priority: Which, for you, comes first: the life or the work? the person (the friendship) or the character (the work *in mente*)?

As Ben continues to report the interaction with Alex in the bar, we read the following sentence: "Alex expressed the intensity of her attention by not touching her water." The syntactical organization of the sentence concedes none of its novelistic qualities to the demands for immediacy that Alex is issuing during their evening together, and implicitly by her posture at this moment. The sentence holds fast to the classic narrative structure that is implicated in her concerns. It is, in other words, what the critic Ann Banfield calls an "unspeakable" sentence. Presence, the immediacy of the personal encounter, is constitutively absent from it; the encounter is subtracted from its environment and converted to a literary morsel for a third party, the reader. Banfield mostly presents this quality of narrative sentences in positive terms: for example, as a "release" of language "from the tyranny of the communicative function," or the impossibility that a novelist could "write a sentence of narration which is false."

The point I wanted to illustrate in my moment of inspiration did not concern simply the structure of fiction (or of the narrative sentence). I especially did not want to encourage any casual acceptance, in my students, of Alex's indictment of fiction for its deficit of "presence." My interest was rather in the scandal that the category of fiction creates for everything and everyone that comes into contact with it—beginning, perhaps, with a character from the first work we had read on the course, the principal addressee and inamorato of Chris Kraus's epistolary, supposedly autobiographical novel *I Love Dick* (1997).

When, at the end of Kraus's work, Dick finally replies to the outpouring of amorous communications from Chris in a heartfelt letter to Chris's husband Sylvère, regretting the style and abruptness of their approach to him on the grounds that friendship "is a delicate and rare thing that's built up over time and is predicated on mutual trust, mutual respect, reciprocal interest and shared commitments," the implication is that Chris and Sylvère entered his life under false pretenses, i.e., were not truly present in their interactions with him. When Dick acknowledges Chris's "talent as a writer," but adds, "I do not share your conviction that my right to privacy has to be sacrificed for the sake of that talent," the conception of talent he is invoking is of something that exists prior to any encounter or production, of whose existence a work may provide evidence, but that is in principle independent of it, and could be expressed in numerous possible forms, practices and situations. Talent, in other words, is a category of "presence."

It's easy to sympathize with Dick. His letter is "reasonable" and "sincere," and Chris reproduces it unchanged (although the contraction "that's" is one of Kraus's stylistic tics). Everything, in other words, has been arranged so that Dick can make his case for the violation of his privacy (that is, for the invasion of his "presence" by Chris and Sylvère's "nonpresence") in full control of his discourse and of its presentation—with no interference, framing commentary, or mediation by Chris. The text of his letter all but concludes the book.

Sympathy for Dick rests on the category of presence. To express sympathy for Dick presumes that he is modeled on a real person, that the letters Chris addresses to him—and the letter from Dick that is reproduced in the work—have their basis and point of reference in a real exchange, that declarations of love (albeit of an ambiguous nature) were made to a person whose privacy was thereby violated, and that the characters of Chris and Sylvère in some sense "correspond" to the author and her husband. *I Love Dick* introduces the question of presence into the novel by rendering its own fictional status ambiguous, partly through a self-styled practice of "naming names."

And yet, in the passage where the phrase "naming names" occurs, Kraus's narrator makes it clear that presence is a fallacy not of practices of writing that use real names, but of those that, under the guise of "fictionalization," preserve an implicit hierarchy between the writing subject and his or her material. Naming names destroys the hierarchy, which is, of course, gendered:

> Because most "serious" fiction, still, involves the fullest possible expression of a single person's subjectivity, it's considered crass and amateurish not to "fictionalize" the

supporting cast of characters, changing names and insignificant features of their identities. The "serious" contemporary hetero-male novel is a thinly veiled Story of Me, as voraciously consumptive as all of patriarchy. While the hero/anti-hero explicitly *is* the author, everybody else is reduced to "characters." [. . .]

When women try to pierce this false conceit by naming names because our "I's" are changing as we meet other "I's," we're called bitches, libellers, pornographers and amateurs.

The "false conceit" is fictionalization itself. We don't need the assumption of a real life model, external to the fiction, in order to identify an ideology of presence in the work. All we need, to use a phrase of the literary critic Alex Woloch's, is the supposition of an "implied human personality" behind the limited "narrative space allocated to a particular character." All we need, in other words, are the standard premises of fiction, as summarized in one of the canonical works of twentieth-century literary criticism, Ian Watt's *The Rise of the Novel* (1957): that the novel is "a full and authentic report of human experience"; the "individuality of the actors concerned"; the "particulars of the times and places of their actions"; and a "largely referential use of language." These formulations take for granted that the work is the expression of a subject; that the subject has something to say; that he or she is well-intentioned in speaking; that the setting, characters, and plot have a vehicular relation to that expression; and that the vehicle or medium is accessible to interpretation by an equally well-intentioned reader with professional expertise, or natural perspicacity. But while fiction, as a literary genre, may be predicated on these assumptions, it was becoming apparent to me that *fictionality*, a quality doubtless embodied in works of fiction, poses a threat to those same assumptions, and that the threat becomes real when fictionality is introduced into the vicinity of any referential discourse—as it cannot fail to be, for example, when the novelist decides to "name names"; or conversely, when the critic (or philosopher or historian) imagines a rhetorical solution to his or her dissatisfaction with the limits of professional discourse that involves their violation. No statement, utterance, or discourse can be brushed by the logic of fictionality and retain its authority—which is, after all, nothing other than the assurance that it speaks in its own voice.

My own critical and political sympathies were not with Dick, nor with Ben's friend Alex, nor, indeed, with the individual I was referring to using the first person pronoun, who felt uneasy in the company of his fiction-writing friend and who now stood at the front of the classroom narrating that sense of unease. My sympathies lay in a different place altogether, a place that it was tempting to identify with the other party in each pairing: with Kraus's "Chris," Lerner's "Ben," and my fiction-writing friend, Joanna Howard. But "sympathy" was not the right word for this new affinity. The feeling was rather of bemusement and enchantment; and what I was bemused and enchanted by was the "scandal"—the scandal that fiction introduces into presence. No reader's sympathy, then, but a sense of "release"—no less—from identification with any such envelope of presence, including myself. Fictionality introduces a seam of uncertainty into every adjacent discourse. Once such uncertainty has been opened up, the subjectivity of the discourse in question is not easily reconstituted.

I wanted my statement to do justice to the scandal. The problem was that the scandal was incompatible with the composition and dissemination of any such statement. And yet, the tendencies in American writing, involving the emancipation and deregulation of fictionality, tendencies that seemed to announce the passing of an era of authoritative criticism, also implied that criticism might locate and give expression to a fictionality that was inherent to it—that, perhaps, it had hitherto been forced to suppress!

Writing in 1966, Michel Foucault imagined a future "breakthrough to a language from which the subject is excluded" —a language, and a thought, in which neither the category of fiction nor that of commentary would enjoy any independent status. Such a language could be "glimpsed," he wrote, in the work of a number of "marginal" figures in the history of literature and philosophy, most notably Maurice Blanchot. The task of defining and comprehending such a language, he acknowledged, had not yet become pressing. Half a century later, perhaps, the lesson of writers such as Chris Kraus and Ben Lerner is that the moment the task of definition and comprehension becomes pressing is the moment it becomes impossible. The real thought of such writing, as Foucault wrote of Blanchot's work, has "withdrawn into the manifestation of [the] work." In a logic that is simultaneously formal, social, and historical, thought in literature escapes all enigmaticalness and achieves a perfect coincidence with what is said, while criticism, for its part, must discover a new relation with its own fictionality to retain its relevance.

6
Statements
Christian Bök

About Plagiarists

"Uncopyrightable" is the longest word in English to use each of its letters no more than once. Prohibitions against the copying of a text now resemble cults of "aniconism," in which zealots must punish anyone who might dare to draw the likeness of a god. Plagiarism makes criminals of us all, for we cannot write if we do not dare to erase the trademark of ownership from every voice, including our own. Imitation is the sincerest flatterer of imitation. Whenever a plagiarist steals my work, I just berate the culprit in public by requoting the greatest of all my epigrams: "Bad poets deface what they take!" Those who cannot learn from poetry are condemned to repeat it. When plagiarizing a text, always steal from the rich. When stealing a text, never leave any trace of your crime, not even the theft of the item. All copyists envy the first genius, just as all admirals envy the first pirate. Do not underplay the fact that the word "underplay" is pig Latin for "plunder." Do not forget that the verb "to publish" derives from the Latin word *publicare*, meaning "to prostitute" and "to confiscate." If you deign to steal my words, then you must also admit to their value. If you are a naysayer who despises me, then you must requote me, to tell the world why you hate me—but alas, I never have to requote you.

About Duchampians

What *Fountain* by Marcel Duchamp has become for artists of the last century, the space-probe Voyager 1 by NASA is going to become for artists of the next century. If we teleport a pissoir backward in time (say 5000 years into the past), the mystery of its manufacture might induce such wonderment in a primordial civilization that the hierophants there must enshrine this porcelain vessel in a sacred space, like a temple. If we teleport a pissoir forward in time (say 5000 years into the future), the history of its significance might induce such wonderment in a superhuman civilization that the scientists there must enshrine this porcelain vessel in a sacred space, like a museum. In both cases, the patina of deep time can turn such a humble vessel into a sacred object. A modern artist who displays the pissoir on a plinth in a gallery has offered us a speculation: "If this thing exists as a work of art, before its time in the past, and if this thing also exists as a work of art, ahead of its time in the future—why not simply call this thing a work of art right now?" A readymade, however, cannot rival the beauty of the Golden Record aboard Voyager 1, for no artwork on Earth can yet persist for billions of years in the hope of addressing an alien mind that might exist in orbit about an alien star.

About Readerships

Avant-garde manifestoes always imply one premise of success: *Oderint dum legant*—"Let them hate us, so long as they read us." Conceptual literature, by comparison, has acquired its readership in part by telling readers that, to like the work, they do not have to read the work. Conceptual literature prefers, instead, to foster a "thinkership" rather than a readership. Only proofreaders need to peruse our books. Only skeptics and acolytes might ever have to verify our claims about the merits of our poetry. Let us not, however, forget that such a concept of writing has also spawned an "unthinkership" of reactionaries (be they philistinic poets or puritanical poets), all of whom prefer the security of "groupthink" rather than the fortuity of iconoclasm. The naysayers, afflicted with *ressentiment*, claim that, because we now enjoy cultural prestige, we must have "sold out" to the market (wherein the success of one clique must come at the expense of all others). Not until the advent of conceptual literature, however, has any avant-garde movement given away its entire *oeuvre* for free to its readers. We steal information from officialdom, then return these documents to the public domain—much like office-clerks, dumping photocopiers at a fire sale. As with any such gift: "It's the thought that counts."

About Philistines

Philistines presume that, in literature, the Egotistical Sublime must always outlaw Negative Capability. Philistines presume that the self must conform to itself, speaking for its own identity in no other voice but its own—i.e. the sincere voice of a witness in the dock, vowing to utter a truth earned under duress. Philistines presume that to speak in any other voice constitutes a betrayal of identity, tantamount to a crime (be it a fraud or a theft)—an act, not of empathy, but of cruelty, committed by a fake self, both untrue and impure. Avant-garde poets have always extolled Negative Capability—but lately they have demanded its abolition, describing such "selflessness" as "irresponsible." Avant-garde poets now use the word "irresponsible" as a euphemism for *Entartete,* condemning the "degenerate" poetics of more famous rivals, who abjure these values of both the true self and the pure self. Avant-garde poets have now adopted illiberal attitudes towards poetry, preferring to take offense at its rebels rather than to give offense to its prudes. Poetry!—be irresponsible. Leave work and duty to the killjoys. Grant play and risk to the brigands. After all, you cannot protect your freedom by making yourself inoffensive to your enemies. You must answer all your foes with the phrase: "My poem, my whim."

About Hatemongers

Hatemongers are fans in disguise, expending attention upon a work, just like any other devotee. Writers who hate their peers are either philistinic (resenting a perceived lack of talent) or puritanical (resenting a perceived lack of virtue). Writers who cannot lay claim to their talent always lay claim to their virtue. People of the future love you for your skill, not for your piety. Virtue is for priests; talent is for artists. Unlike deeds, ideas have now become dangerous, not because they can cause actual injury to others, but only because they can get a thinker into trouble. Poets of virtue with no talent always argue that poets of talent have neither. Poets who denounce their peers for "wrongthink" compromise the aesthetic liberties of everyone. The avant-garde now believes that, when offended, the self achieves a state of grace. The avant-garde has now become a brand of *ressentiment*, finding fault with the talent that it envies in others. Any innovation in poetry is a gimmick or a misstep, only if you are not the first to have tried it yourself. The edginess of a poem is always much too dull to cause anybody harm. The autocratic, the censorious, are never social, always unjust. The mob metaphorically "lynches" the poet for using the word "lynches" metaphorically. No readers need your permission to think for themselves.

About Instigators

Conceptual literature strives to replace the expressive intentions of the self with a whole array of, apparently impossible, poetic values, arguing for styles of poetry, dismissed by skeptics as uncreative, unoriginal, uninspired, even uneventful. Such poets resort to a diverse variety of anti-expressive, anti-discursive strategies (including the use of copied texts, forced rules, opaque marks, and even cyborg tools), doing so in order to explore the limit-cases of the readymade text, the mannerist text, the illegible text, and the aleatoric text—all considered "unliterary." When younger writers remark upon the liberal, emotive benefit gained from the act of creation itself, their platitudes seem therapeutic, if not sentimental, in the face of such limit-cases. I do not think that creativity arises from a transcendent, metaphysical desire to be either expressive or generative; instead, I think that any act of creativity responds to a vexatious, aesthetic shortcoming in the world at large—a shortcoming that no one else seems to be redressing on our behalf, and consequently we must redress this shortcoming for ourselves. I think that, for this reason, I write poetry, not because I feel innately "creative" or innately "artistic," but because no other poet in the world seems to be writing the kind of book that I might want to read.

About Malingerers

Emotions are not skilled workers. Poetry is no longer language on vacation, but language on furlough—unemployed, as if by a layoff, yet unwilling to reenter the workforce. Poetry thus commits a kind of welfare fraud upon us all. Poetry lets you do the wrong thing with anything so long as anything is language. Poetry has become a distant factory, where robots manufacture nothing but sparks. Verse may "serve" what we mean; or verse may "sever" what we mean—but alas, it always veers away from what we mean to mean. Look upon my Despair, ye Mighty—and work! Give a man a poem, and he will starve for a day, but teach a man to be a poet, and he will starve for a lifetime. Rats, electroshocked after pressing a lever, never again press it—but the poet still composes couplets. The best poem, to me, is most like a telephone, ignored, but ringing, inside a clear, solid cube of quartz. The office has now become the most advanced frontier of writing (turning poets into agents of both word processing and data management). The purpose of poetry is to fill out forms. And from form to form, we morph. We trade our dithyrambs for algorithms. Do not compose lyrics; do not recount stories. Do not confess to being something so boring as a person in love: write like an amoeba, a meteor, or an abacus.

About Postmortems

Nothing ever expires in any of the "dead ends" of poetry. Every *cul de sac* is a Petri dish for novelty. When naysayers say: "Poetry is dead!"—I just respond by building an unkillable poem. Like asymptotes, aesthetic movements never quite reach the limits of their own demise. The prefix "post-" can no longer imply an advancement beyond, or even an abandonment of, some past idea about literature; instead, the prefix now signifies something like: "More of the same!—only worse." The prefix "post-" might not indicate the foreclosure of a literary movement, so much as the prefix might indicate an impatience that, despite all efforts to the contrary, we have yet to surpass such a movement—and thus we must pretend to have done so, long before we have actually produced a more advanced paradigm to replace it. The prefix "neo-" is always more retro than novel. The word "new" signifies nothing more than a digital upgrade to the software of ideology. New and improved!—twice as many adjectives. The avant-garde has now stooped to promote the schlock of the new. To add the prefix "post-" to a concept is like trying to destroy a beloved toy, because you envy the first child to have played with it. No verse must be averse to anything more novel than itself. A novel is anything but.

7
Just Try
Julie Carr

A series of experiments precedes my writing and demands that I experiment in response. Here are just four such experiments:

1. Within seven months of President Ronald Reagan's inauguration in 1981, Congress slashed spending by $35 billion and reduced personal and corporate income taxes by $37.7 billion. "About $25 billion in cuts—some 70 percent of the budget savings—were made in programs affecting the poor."
2. "Federal housing assistance was reduced unmercifully during the 1980s. In 1981 the Department of Housing and Urban Development had budget authorizations of $32.2 billion; by 1989 they had been slashed to a mere $6.9 billion—a reduction of 78 percent."[1]
3. In 2010, guns took the lives of 31,076 Americans in homicides, suicides and unintentional shootings. This is the equivalent of more than 85 deaths each day and more than three deaths each hour.[2] Over the past two decades, the number of people with concealed carry permits has climbed from under 5 million to 12.8 million,[3] as now every state in the nation allows concealed carry, with twelve of those states now not even requiring a permit.[4]

---

[1] https://object.cato.org/pubs/pas/pal127.pdf
[2] http://smartgunlaws.org/facts/statistics/
[3] https://newyorker.com/magazine/2016/06/26/after-orlando-examining-the-gun-business
[4] http://smartgunlaws.com

4.

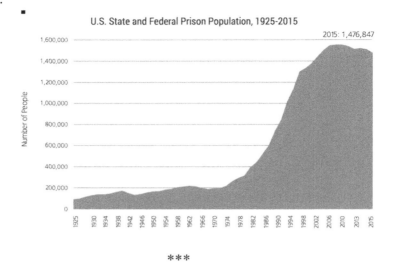

U.S. State and Federal Prison Population, 1925-2015

***

How does writing respond to such experiments that take human life, and the barest of imperatives for care, as their material?

WHAT DO YOU OWN? WHAT OWNS YOU?

One cannot write, I then thought and said, without prison statistics in mind at all times.

And then, with such statistics in mind, do we write more or do we write less? Do we mention the cat tumbling down the stone stairs, or do we not? Do we include something called "play" or do we avoid it? These are the questions of real life. If the greatest, by which I mean largest, installation project called "What do you own? What owns you?" is underway right now all over the country, how would we become its visitors?

***

These are the questions of real life.

If I am to write at all, it's only to experiment in how to record and respond to such questions.

From Labor Day 2011 to Labor Day 2013 I wrote every day, only reading back what I had written after three-month-long periods of writing. These "read back" sessions lasted just 3 days and could involve only the most minimal editing (fixing spelling and adjusting spacing). This way, for two years, I tried to keep myself in the space of the unknown. I did not want my writing to become in any way domesticated. I did not want to think I knew what I was doing. I wrote, in a sense, into the future, because only in the future would I allow myself to become familiar with the writing.

A LITERARY TEXT AS AMORPHOUS AS POSSIBLE, WHICH NEVER TAKES SHAPE

On July 24, stars fell down wells, becoming an owl's jewly
    eyes.
On August 6, the poet put his penis on the tumblr page.
Wind / leaves / wind / leaves / wind / lives / leave / delve /
    in wind
The word "blown" cannot mean much to a child, but
    everything always ends up otherwise, O lovely
    stranger.
The sun, an engrossing inglorious pulp. The abstracted
    buildings, stitched up by sleep.
This drink is strange, making itself known
in our throats.

***

Such wildness was not courted, however, for its own sake. Rather, what was wild and unknowable, strange and frightening in the world/country/neighborhood/house/self could only be accessed, it seemed, through the dare I'd given myself: to remain as open as possible to the actual. Eventually, I called the project REAL LIFE: AN INSTALLATION.

***

In the days or weeks or months after December 14, 2012, a slow and broken series of internal and external observations eventually formed a numbered sequence I called "Break: Silence in 20 Pieces":

4.

The boy handed me my change in the parking lot. It was precisely 9 hours after the killing. He saw my face.

"I hope you have a good rest of your day." No hope for the first part. It was five in the afternoon. Cloudy, windy, cold.

8.

Today I was hoping to escape the bare language of fact. But is it too late for complexities and games?

The yard holds its whiteness, witness.

fallow-pleasures

Graves prepared, entered, complete. They will show us
        the faces of the murdered children, but not

of their mothers and fathers.

***

To say that the writing was experimental is only to say that the world was. In one state in our country, they experimented with making it illegal to feed the hungry. In another, a cop experimented with making public his most terrifying desires:

SPACE IS THE MUSIC OF THE UNSUNG

As we also recall if we are able that in the two thousandth and fourteenth year of our lord, also the Hebrew year of 5775 and the Islamic year of 1436, a man in the ninth decade of his life on earth, residing in the State of Florida, formerly the Spanish colony La Florida, and prior to that the land of the Seminole, was three times cuffed and three times taken down and three times fined for feeding chicken and cheesy potatoes to strangers with no steady home.

NETWORKED CUNT

In the colo-

rado radio flash

the cop blogs his desire to eat women's

flesh.

I wrote the phrase: *intractable enigma.*

The soul is united only with itself.

***

Then in a park right nearby a company experimented with giving away ammunition rounds to anyone:

THE CODEPENDENCY OF MOURNING AND HOPE

Tomorrow at Infinity Park ammunitions manufacturer Magpul will be giving away 30-round magazines to the first 1,500 people who show up. All you have to be is 18 to get one. "That sort of thing never happens here," says the neighbor of the two dead little boys. Yes it does.

The phrase

semblance shattered

                       ***

After the two years had passed, I had over 600 pages of material to work with. I began, then, a process of editing that took, all told, three years of often interrupted (by other writing projects) dedication. What emerged from this experiment was a series of forms, or perhaps better put, approaches. Form or pattern, what Gerard Manley Hopkins called "oftening, over-and-overing, aftering," comes in to make breathing space in the chaotic swarm of information, desires, boredoms, fears, pleasures and confusions that might be said to make up the real life of any one person. One of these "oftenings" was the dreamed or imagined art installation.

TWO DREAM INSTALLATIONS ON PRACTICE

My neighbor and I decide to create a commune made up of dancers, artists, and activists. But first we must train them. We gather them into a room and we begin a long, slow dance. The purpose of the dance is to teach people how to support one another and to be supported. Therefore there's a lot of falling, catching, and lifting. When the dance is over I say, "Tomorrow's dance will be a lot more precise." What I have in mind involves touching one another's arms and hands—examining with all of our senses the split second between not touching and touching.

The kids and I are in someone else's apartment. The person who lives there is not home. We are looking through the rooms with urgency: opening drawers and cabinets, lifting objects from desks and countertops, staring at photographs, reading mail. We are, it seems, trying to find the person by examining all of their belongings. This is something we do regularly. It's a "practice." But in this case, since we ourselves once lived in this apartment, even as we are looking for the other person, we are also looking for ourselves underneath or within that person's things, underneath or within that person.

INSTALLATION: TOPOS

The horse is on the floor. The voice is turned hard. The
    word is smoke.
The quiet woman burns. Horse-witch.

***

I could say that all of writing is experimental, if we think of the word in terms of its Latin root (*experiri*: to try), but am aware that blithe statements like this are not generally that useful. In the history of experimental writing in the US that I know about, the brand has often been considered cold, white, calculating, disengaged, even if (intellectually, at any rate) daring. In the 1990s when I was beginning to become a writer, the experimental was often pitted against the confessional and its on-stage less-white cousin, spoken word, which was warmer, even flushed or hot, bodily and brave. I moved from New York to Berkeley in 2001, thereby veering closer to the chillier of these poles. But now I live in Colorado where it's all good, and I think of my experiments as deeply confessional, my calculated projects heated up with rage, fear, love and the urgent call to in some way respond.

ONCE ONLY AGAIN AND AGAIN

Once only again and again: imagine the morsel, if possible, of Jewish resistance—the charred chair, no windows, more morbid far arrests, the red and the black, the unburied. Once and once again once, a woman comes through the door, pushing her hair back from her face, a hedonistic moment, like poetry night in Glasgow, or like a little seaside town where teenagers film themselves reading from notebooks while sitting on statues in the winter. Imagine, if you can, their flowing flower-eyes, so that you might once and once again address the State with a little mouth full of water.

TRY

Or start again: Only in free movement does the world render itself real.

8
Experimental writing is a condition, not a genre
Jeffrey DeShell

This condition suggests that *experimental* is not an adjective or adverb, and *writing* not a noun.

Experimental does not modify *writing,* as if *writing* were a stable and coherent essence, living happily in the world, only to be destabilized (ruined) by this short-sighted mutation. There is nothing essential about *writing* as such, and nothing secondary, parasitic or supplemental about *experimental*.

Experimental writing does not result *from* or *in* the literary, or even literature itself.

If anything, literature or the literary originates from (in) the experiment of writing.

There is no theory of experimental writing.

There is nothing that can be said from one case to another, from one experiment to another.

Whereas scientific experiments are often attempts to replicate previous results, writing experiments attempt to negate previous outcomes.

To interrupt what has come before.

Experimental writing is the negation of theory, negation of the concept.

Negation is not nothing.

The interruption of narrative.

The narrative of interruption.

If experiments have anything in common, it is the shared possibility of unique failure.

Because experimental writing is not a genre, it doesn't desire to follow a pre-existing blueprint in order to accomplish an external project.
It does not desire to tell us what we (writer and/or reader) already know.
It is (invokes) desire for the unforeseen.
It is (performs) desire for an other.

What *is* experimental writing?
What *does* experimental writing *do*?
These are the wrong questions.

Because experimental writing is not a genre, its success or failure cannot be determined by external criteria.
Criteria such as popularity, influence, historical significance, historical accuracy, reading groups, celebrity status, classroom adoption, retweets, reviews, sales figures, page views, focus groups, emotional resonance, crowdsourcing, movie options, etc., have no bearing on experimental writing.
What then?

Experimental writing is the putting-into-play.
Of what?
Of the uncontrollable play of language, its freedom and joy, its ecstasy and apostasy.
Against/with the attempt to give this language form.
Some other words for form:
Grammar
Syntax
Narrative
Prosody
Meaning.

Language without form is impossible (Stein, Beckett).

Form without play is abstract, sterile (a dominant misreading of Western theology).

To put into play in order to create the unforeseen.
The unresolvable creating the unforeseeable.
To put difference into play in order to create the different.
To create other than the same.

The ethics of experimental writing.
To be absolutely open for whatever may come.
To be absolutely open for an other.

Such experiments demand self-difference, alienation, auto-negation.
Rigorous ecstasy.
To be open to the other you have to become other.
To yourself.
To put language and form into play
Means to put yourself into play.
Absolutely.

This putting into play is not immediate, timeless, easily accomplished.
It is one of the most difficult things imaginable.
It requires time and work. A lifetime.
Of sacrifice.
The writer *pays* attention (O'Connor, Weil).
Emphasis on the verb.
Emphasis on the cost.

This openness to the other, to the self become other (Kafka's definition of a writer), is necessarily terrifying and painful.
Liquefying and liquidating.
"The axe for the frozen sea within us."
"'Be just' it says."
Etc.

This is saying too little.

The insertion of the other('s narrative) into narrative is necessarily violent, necessarily critical, necessarily monstrous.
What can happen when anything can happen?

The other can come from anywhere.
At any time.

Experimental writing is not a genre, and is therefore not historical.
Hysterical yes.

Experimental writing is not a genre and therefore cannot be determined by lists:
Of writers
Of works
Of dates
Of journals
Of publishers.

Of experiences.

There's no development, no timeline, no taxonomy, no hierarchy of better or worse, no questions of quality, no sub-genres or further designations. It's not a matter of determining what example fits best into what model, or how one artifact proceeds from another, or what social or political environment leads to the production of what writing. It's not a question of Realism or a deviation from Realism (Realism is the deviation). It's not a problem of techniques or strategies. It's not a question of schools or other groupings, or actions or reactions, culture high or low. It's not a question of colonialism, postcolonialism, decolonialism or neocolonialism, nor of democracy or elitism, patriarchy or matriarchy. It's not a question of style or voice.
Or of languages.
Or gender.
Or of technology.
Certainly not a question of universalism. Thank God we are not the same.
It is not a question of structure.

Or of craft.

Or any of these inadequate metaphors, wrung from material or conceptual systems, which signify a desire to domesticate experimental writing into either the mundane or the philosophical. Or both.

It's never a question of determining what experimental is and what it is not.

Experimental writing is indifferent to such descriptions or definitions.

Experimental writing is indifference itself.

Indifferent to everything but difference.

How to prepare for the truly unknown?

With and to the limits of the imagination.

With irony.

Not North American irony, the superficial irony composed of sentimentality, sarcasm, smugness and sincerity. The irony of TV and the indulgent memoir.

But a more basic, fundamental and irrecuperable irony, an irony of Albertine's bedroom and Kleist's puppets.

Of hoodoo and the fast red road.

Of bass riddim and Five Spice Street.

Of "Open paragraph" and "barking in a fit of laughter, obscene and touching."

Etc.

A *gelassenheit* without transcendence.

A *sabot* thrown into the dialectical machine.

A detachment without passivity.

A separation demonstrating the propinquity of all.

This irony does not spring from or lead to quietude, tranquility, inaction.

To pay attention, to open oneself to the other *as* other

Can be read as political actions *par excellence.*

If necessary.

But these actions require patience to unfold.

Patience not to confuse images of the same with possibilities of the other.

Patience to refuse the temptations of immediate understanding and instantaneous comprehension in order to open oneself toward genuine alterity.

In time.

Patience to experience.

In time.

An active ethics, temporal but not historical.

With everything at stake.

Everything.

"Writing is fighting."

And what of responsibility?

To the reader?

The writer?

The text itself?

The world we live in?

The world to come?

Responsibility is the ability to respond.

To be responsible to is to provide the possibility for response.

The possibilities of response necessarily include the possibilities of silence.

9
Experimental Theory
Jeffrey R. Di Leo

Theory is stronger and more experimental now than it ever was in the twentieth century. The reason for this is not necessarily a deepening or intensification of the work of theory in traditional areas such as literary criticism and critique (though arguments may be made here), but rather a widening or broadening of its reach and domain.

Theory today is a multi- and inter-disciplinary endeavor that operates within and among the humanities (particularly, history, languages, linguistics, the arts, philosophy and religion in addition to literature), the social sciences (including anthropology, ethnic and cultural studies, economics, political science, psychology, and sociology), and many of the professions (for example, architecture, business, communication, education, environmental studies, journalism, law, museum studies, media studies, military science, public policy, and sport science, among others).

In addition to its now somewhat more standard-fare work in these areas, of which prime examples are readily available, it has also made some exciting experimental inroads into the natural sciences (for example, biology, physics, the earth sciences, and the space sciences) and the formal sciences (especially mathematics, computer science, and systems science).

To be sure, more disciplines from across the academy have integrated theory into their practice than at any other time in history—and, in many ways, theory today is the id of the disciplines and the experimental engine of interdisciplinary studies.

Moreover, the academic community that engages, supports, and uses theory in the twenty-first century is not only much larger in number than it ever was in the twentieth century, for many the presumed "heyday of theory," it is also, in part as a consequence of its multi- and inter-disciplinary reach, more diverse with respect to the objects and subjects of its attention.

In addition to traditional objects of theoretical engagement such as literary, philosophical, and artistic texts, many others are now becoming commonplace such as new media, the environment, and even the university itself.

But theory has also extended the range of *subjects* of its attention. In addition to more commonplace ones such as narrative, identity, translation, and rhetoric, subjects such as affect, globalization, biopolitics, political economy, and institutions have emerged as major areas of experimentation for theory today.

The popularity and strength of theory today is directly related to the experimental fearlessness it engenders in individuals and communities to question the precepts and extend the boundaries of individual disciplines as well as to draw the disciplines into dialogue with each other. In addition, theory's willingness to turn its critical powers upon itself proves to be still another point of attraction. This is why there seems to be nary a subject or object that has not been engaged in some way or another by theory today. To be sure, most everything is fair game for theory's experimentation.

If anything has died in the world of theory in the twenty-first century, then it is the dominance of its "-isms." There was a time in the previous century when affiliation with an "-ism" was the required badge of entry into the theory world. One was not just a "theorist," but a member of a specific sub-community of theory designated by an "-ism."

Just as the world of religion has Catholicism, Judaism, and Buddhism, the world of theory had structuralism, Marxism, and feminism. And the lines of division between them within the theory community were at times no less flexible than those within the religious community.

Think about how search committees used to badger job

candidates with parochial questions about their theoretical affiliation? To do so today almost seems like a violation of FERPA laws. And woe be to the job candidate who professed the wrong theoretical affiliation. Or confessed to the right one, but was not in line with the preferred house of postmodernism or version of feminism?

Though the late twentieth century may have been the heyday of "high" theory, in retrospect, it appears much more provincial and doctrinaire compared to the contemporary world of theory— one that is not only much more experimental, pluralistic, and amorphous but also less divisive than the previous one.

Whereas in the past, fault lines between and distinctions within "-isms" often became feuding points among theorists, the new object- or subject-centered world of theory is a much less divisive one. Who today is going to argue that the object or subject of your theoretical affection (say, pop music or affect) is the wrong one? Or that working on "debt" is superior to working on "masculinity"?   Though there is still some bickering about "whose" debt and "which" masculinity is the right, valid, or true one, such complaints seem more reactionary than progressive, scholastic than pluralistic—and ultimately thus less acceptable— after the demise of the big house of new-, post-, and original-flavor "-isms."

Theoretical attention to objects or subjects allows for more experimentation, pluralism, and toleration in the theory world compared to its previous incarnation as a world of schools, movements, and -isms.

Theory never changed tense, it just changed focus. That is, it just became much more experimental. Since the ascent of high theory (or the even higher, so-called "sky-high theory" or "theoreticism") and the emergence of various forms of opposition to it, rumors of and statements about the demise of theory have persisted. Even today, closure regarding the issue seems remote. Just consider the work of Vincent Leitch, who recently published *Literary Theory in the 21st Century: Theory Renaissance* (2014), one of the most robust and enthusiastic defenses of the continuing presence of theory in the twenty-first century.

Leitch acknowledges that word on the street is that theory is dead—superseded by a multitude of studies. Gone are theory stalwarts such as deconstruction, Marxism, and feminism. They have been replaced by studies of everything and anything from Barbie dolls and Beyoncé to biopolitics and books.

Leitch's maintains that there are "94 subdisciplines and fields circling around 12 major topics" in literary and cultural theory today, which he notes are "reminiscent of planets and satellites." Of these ninety-four subdisciplines, fifty include adjectives followed by the noun "studies": patronage, subaltern, working-class, debt, object, technoscience, animal, food, postcolonial, border, diaspora, new American, resistance, surveillance and security, body, cyborg, gender, disability, age, leisure, new Southern US, Whiteness, indigenous, ethnic, women's, queer, masculinity, sexuality, celebrity, fashion, sport, gaming, sound, visual culture, tv, film, periodical, archive, professionalization, canonization, academic labor, literacy, composition, reception, performance, narrative, trauma, memory, and holocaust.

Another twenty clearly imply the noun "studies," but for one reason or another it is not stated. For example, the field "media studies" has eight subdisciplines. All but three ("new media," "social media," and "book history") include the noun "studies"— and for at least two of these ("new media" and "social media") the noun "studies" is clearly implied. The final one, "book history," is probably more accurate with "studies" replacing the noun "history." Among the ninety-four subdisciplines, the noun "theory" is only used twice: in "cognitive theory" and "affect theory."

Clearly, if Leitch is even somewhat accurate in his universal mapping of literary and cultural theory in the twenty-first century, there is little or no room in the new millennium for the more dominant mapping of literary theory and criticism, namely, one which divides it into schools and movements. For Leitch, designators of the theory and criticism universe such as Russian formalism, New Criticism, psychoanalysis, feminism, Marxism, structuralism, poststructuralism, queer theory, New Historicism, and postcolonial theory are strictly a twentieth-century phenomena. Though these designators were important to the emergence of "theory" in the last quarter of the twentieth-century, they have outlived their usefulness for mapping literary and cultural theory in the twenty-first century. The explosion of "studies" in the first quarter of the twenty-first century leaves little opportunity for organizing literary and cultural theory into the older matrix of schools and movements. Or, alternately stated, studies as sub-species of the "twentieth century" schools and movements makes for very messy and confusing mapping. Hence, why bother? Better to just leave it to the historians of theory to trace the legacies of theory amidst the "studies" multitude.

What then to do with "theory," that is, the sum body of the twentieth-century's schools and movements in the wake of the explosion of twentieth-first century studies? Leitch's answer is surprising. Namely, dub the first quarter of the twenty-first century a "theory renaissance." This is the somewhat counter-intuitive task of his book—a task which as difficult as it may sound is one for which he makes an incredibly strong case. In a nutshell, his argument is that all ninety-four subdisciplines and twelve major topics "stem directly from recognizable contemporary schools and movements of theory." Therefore, because there is no other term that adequately captures the "proliferation" charted into ninety-four subdisciplines and twelve major topics, we need to just continue to use the designator "theory."

Leitch's approach to theory in the twentieth century is right on the mark and represents the most energetic response to the so-called "death of theory." Not only is theory not dead, it is undergoing a "renaissance," or better yet, a "reinvention," of sorts. To put it bluntly, the death of theory is an illusion—and the future of this illusion, through efforts such as Leitch's, will hopefully be short-lived.

Still, what happens if we replace all of the uses of "study" in his galaxy with the term "theory" and make its implicit references explicit? For one thing, doing so would end the charade that all of these "studies" are not second-generation theory—or dare we say, "*new* theory"? For transitional purposes, it was important at the end of the twentieth century to designate this work with a term other than theory. But a quarter-century later it just seems silly and is confusing. Theory is not dead—it just changed its name when its focus and the objects of its attention began to change and become the subject of broad *experimentation*.

Calling theory "theory," rather than "studies," allows the larger and committed community dedicated to it to regroup and retool their identity in the wake of major experimentation in the theory world today. It is past time that this was done.

Paraphrasing Mark Twain, "The reports of the death of theory have been greatly exaggerated." Experimental theory represents the best and strongest aspects of theory today. Without it, reports of the death of theory would not be exaggerations.

10
My Deep Zoo
Rikki Ducornet

1. I am six. I keep a robin's egg cradled in cotton. Smashed between the hands of a friend of the family, the egg takes on talismanic properties, provokes a series of sympathies.
2. Alabaster egg once belonging to Werner and Kate Wolff. (Werner Wolff shows up in BRIGHTFELLOW as Verner Vanderloon.) A splash of iron red looks like blood.
3. Chicken fetus, four days old.
4. One version among many (this one a glyph) of Max Ernst's loplop.
5. My version of the LopLop (PHOSPHOR IN DREAMLAND).

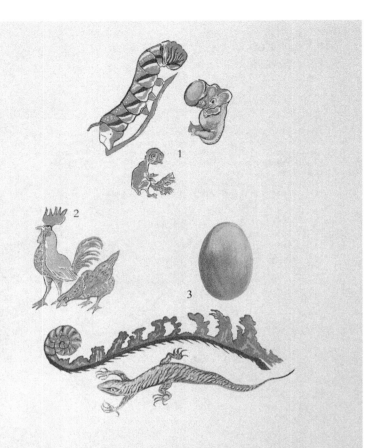

1. The fetus—human and chicken (as are all others, and all else!)—is ruled by restlessness. (MUTABILITY!)

2. Across the street, the chicken yard. Eden of a kind. (The farmer shows me his wondrous stash of anomalies.) (NOTHING IS STILL!)

3. I am eight. Entering the Bard College library alone for the first time, and crossing a bridge of green glass that leads to the second storey stacks, I see the spine of a book the color of my talismanic murdered egg—an irrestible soft turquoise. Written by Paul Éluard and illustrated by Max Ernst, the book is MISFORTUNES OF THE IMMORTALS. It teaches me about eternal enigmas and perfected memories. And it is ruled by birds. (It is already haunted by THE LOPLOP!)

1. A leaping hare, her fur ignited by the setting sun, enters my dream and in this way sparks THE
   STAIN and all that follows. (The work is spawned and/or overseen by dreams.)
2. One persistent, snowy winter, a red fox walks me to the school bus. A previous summer, a dead red
   fox, its belly swarming with yellow jackets, had revealed that the world is simultaneously beautiful
   and terrible. (ALCHEMY!)
3. A bumblebee's sting ignites not only the letter B (BUZZ), but the entire alphabet. It convinces me
   of what I think I already knew—that life's intention is the searching out of the fertile passages and
   places, a fearless looking for the thorny A and B in everything.

Deep Zoo Excerpts

The shapes of time are the prey we want to capture.
—George Kubler, *The Shape of Time*

When I was a child, I came upon the dead body of a red fox in the woods; it was early summer, and the fox's belly was burning brightly with yellow bees. A species of animate calligraphy, the bees rose and fell in a swarm that revealed, then concealed, the corpse. Yellow and black they tigered it, and they glamorized it too—transforming what otherwise might have seemed horrible into a thing of rare beauty. It is no accident that my first novel opens with the death of a creature in a wood.
—*The Deep Zoo*

. . .

When I was a small child, our nearest neighbor—and he was a poultry farmer—candled eggs for me. One by one the eggs surrendered their opacity and, should they have one, revealed their secret. In this way the farmer knew when the yolks were doubled, and it would have pleased him to hand me a box of twelve such prodigies. Sometimes the candle revealed a spot of blood or a nascent chick rooted to the yolk like a tiny fiddlehead fern rolled up upon itself. In this way, I saw how in the beginning an animal is a kind of plant.

My first childhood room—and its floor was covered in deep blue linoleum—looked out on the meadow where our neighbor's chickens meandered and sometimes managed to perch in the low-growing trees. Stretched out on the linoleum, I contemplated another mystery, which protracted the delicious experience of candling: a hollow Easter egg made of hard white sugar and provided with a thimble-sized diorama. I recall gazing for hours with longing at an idealized version of my window view: a miniature meadow in which a hen sat with her chicks in what seemed to be perfect silence and kindness. The paradise contained within the sugar egg cast a spell within the room and extended to the chicken yard across the street; it too was silent and ordered in my mind. Even now, and although I know it is impossible, the chicken yard is as still as a museum diorama, and as mysterious. Mysterious because it is the first landscape I pondered. Mysterious as the little wood behind the house rife with sumac and garter snakes and skunkweed and red foxes. And there was a song I loved then about a fox who goes out on a dark and stormy night to raid a chicken coop and bring a chicken dinner back to his family, who wait for him in the lair. The refrain went something like this:

> And the little ones gnawed on the bones, O!
> The bones O, the bones O!
> And the little ones chewed on the bones!

The meadow, its hundreds of white birds, the sumac, the foxes, the neighbor's kitchen, his gentle hand holding up a candled egg for me to see—all of these are held in thrall behind the glass of memory. And like a magic lantern image projected within a darkened room, they appear in isolation from everything else. One's childhood is like that dark room, illuminated by the most precious, the most incongruous things!

One morning the neighbor showed me his treasure: a two-headed chick kept in a jelly jar and floating in alcohol. This memory is dynamic and allows me to recall what it was to be six years old, fully alive and sparked by something strange and terrifying and beautiful. The two-headed chick is perpetually stimulating because it is the first event in a series of events that sparked my imagination in a novel, an unsettling, and so, salutary manner. As did the linoleum I have mentioned, which, in the shadows of evening, became an unfathomable sea of indigo water studded with yellow islands barely large enough to stand on. Tiptoeing across that linoleum, I risked my life. I knew that the thread that anchored me to the world was as delicate as the thread that anchored the forming chick to its yolk. And I had seen how the monstrous could surge forth unexpectedly from a thing as prosaic as an egg. The two-headed chick was the indication of questions I could not even begin to ask, and like the shadow games I played each evening on the linoleum, it offered a sprawl of fantasy and a troublous delight. I think it trained me in a certain kind of looking.

To look at the anomalous chick was to be given access to something precious, which, in the half-light of evening, took on a kind of substance and immediacy. This something precious had all to do with reverie, a restless imagining. The yellow islands were all the islands of the mind burning brightly in the safety of my own private darkness. They were places of essential and dangerous beauty—dangerous because they were somehow forbidden, anomalous, maybe truly monstrous. The linoleum games offered also a taste of infinity because they disrupted categories and suggested new ones. In the shadows of my room, I lived in the land of conjecture.

When one is six, many questions cannot be asked because they cannot be formulated let alone intimated.

Two years pass; it is summer and there are eight of us. We play pirates, Clue, cops and robbers, Old Maid, games of Goose, poker, cowboys and Indians, and the games of our own invention. We play at hide-and-seek, and I pride myself on the fact that I am hard to find. The year is 1951, and Senator McCarthy's brand of obscurification is packing steam. Our fathers are college professors, and we are aware that the lethalities of the moment might possibly reach us, as might the fallout from Russian nuclear devices. There is the threat of Martians and, to a lesser degree, vampires. The brother of a classmate has been crippled by polio, and another child has drowned. Shadows, then, of one kind and another. Our knowledge of the world is both intimate—the campus where our fathers teach, the woods, the Hudson River—and vastly incomplete. But as I am about to discover, the essential things that are kept from children will manage to surge into the day. And it may even be that the darkness is a place of safekeeping.

So. The game is hide-and-seek, and the afternoon is on the wane. We scatter and I run into a vacant lecture hall—which is surely cheating—and up three flights of stairs. At the end of a dim corridor is an unlocked door, and suddenly I find myself standing in a beautiful room, spacious, its ceiling impossibly high—so high it seems the room has its own atmosphere. In fact, the air in that room smells strange, not familiar at all; not quite terrestrial. Recently I came upon an obscure reference to a room where the angels—and I don't believe in angels—were said to receive their instructions. In my memory, this room seems a likely place. Because I am about to find what I have, unaware, been seeking. It is the one thing each child—the child who has only recently left her tail, her gills behind—seeks. The human child who is always as eager to encounter a turtle as she is a tiger or a triceratops—because she knows (and her knowledge is innate and intimate) that they are all her tribe.

Imagine a vast rectangular room, its west wall taken up with vertiginous windows. In the east the sun hangs high above the roof, and the room is heavy with shadows. The entire east wall is taken up with cabinets fronted with glass; glass spills to the floor like heavy water. The cabinets are old and pocked with bubbles; the glass is of uneven thickness. Like the restless objects of desire that elude Alice's eyes in the sheep's shop in Wonderland, the things in the cabinet are both appealing and enigmatic.

The sun slides down a notch and then another. And like an animated ink, the shadows within the cabinet begin to leak; they recede. The sun slides down another notch. Light floods the room and in that white air the objects within the cabinet catch fire. They twinkle.

Now imagine that you see sideral space clearly chartered. It is as if peering down a black hole you see your own face reflected in a pool. The most essential knowledge, until then glimpsed within the candled egg and the jelly jar, perceived but never before truly considered, hangs suspended in an ordered sequence—star after luminous star.

Look: here is the modular chicken, the entire progress of its gestation bared to the eye, and here: a fetal cat in levitation. To the left a single natal lizard, and above, one preliminary lamb. All this announces the greatest treasure of all: the dizzying itinerary of the human fetus; it rides the afternoon across an entire shelf. Each and every one of its gestures is expressive and luminous. And we are privileged; we are looking at the alphabet of sparks that spell the world. Some are as mute as water, some hiss like fire, some respire: this is the breath that reconciles water and fire. Here are all the points of departure: an alphabet of eyes, of the organs of speech, the five places of the human mouth, the 231 formations made tangible out of the intangible air. The one name, the one flame that cannot stand still; clairvoyance, the small intestines like seaweed floating toward the beach; the child's face cut from fresh clay with a knife of green leaves; the lotus flower upon which Buddha sits; a serpent at the world's edge, the embodiment of time's passage, the twelve constellations, the twelve organs of the body. All that had been baffling, hermetic, unfolds, exquisitely palpable. And we know, without a doubt, that the ark is contained within each of us.

—from *The Practice of Obscurity*

. . .

Imagine with me a book that, like a seed held in the reader's hands, under her gaze, *effloresces*. A book that contains not only other books, a library, the world's library—a pleasure already almost ours—but a book that, like a living organism, evolves in unique and unexpected ways. A book whose every mutation persists in space and rides the air. That, like the chrysalis, explodes on the scene in new and dynamic forms with each reading. It is thought that whales sing their world into visibility and so: meaning, stereoptically. Let us acknowledge how their songs extend and enliven our own. Imagine with me a book that, like those gardens of Osiris and Adonis once so beloved of the Egyptians and the Greeks, is the place where Eros sleeps and dreams, and awakens again and again. A book that, as it surfaces, respires . . .

—from *Books of Natural and Unnatural Nature*

11
Notes on Experimental Writing
Brian Evenson

A few years ago, a colleague of mine guest-edited an annual anthology of experimental writing. It was a good, smart anthology, but—largely because over the course of a dozen years I had taken her reading recommendations, been to dozens of readings, and had been trained to a particular way of thinking about experimental and innovative writing—it held few surprises or discoveries for me. I could almost guess from reading the table of contents what experimental would consist of. I hadn't read all the writers, but I'd read at least something by most of them. As a result, apart from one or two notable exceptions, I found the anthology more often comforting rather than startling: it affirmed my understanding of what one strand of experimental writing was.

Then another, newer colleague guest-edited the next volume of the same annual. I settled in to read it, prepared for a similarly benign experience.

Only it didn't work that way. I didn't recognize nearly as many writers, and the writers I did recognize had work quite different from what I was used to from them. There was a larger percentage of prose, and a different range of voices and presses were represented. Every time I began to feel I knew what this anthology was up to, what version of "experimental" it was postulating, I would hit a piece that would cause me to rethink or reformulate my understanding. Rather than affirming my sense of what "experimental" was, this second anthology challenged and expanded it.

I'm not saying one anthology was objectively better than

the other—and, indeed, I can easily imagine, had my training been different, being more surprised by the first than by the second. But one was more necessary, and more experimental, for me, at a particular moment. Ultimately, experiment should be something that reveals something new to us, challenges us as readers, not something that affirms our sense of what writing is. Which suggests the experimental nature of a piece is highly dependent on the particularities of a given reader.

***

There is still work that surprises me, still work that can astound, but it is rarely what others recommend to me as "innovative" or "experimental." How often am I surprised when reading a writer who I already admire? I enjoy the work, am impressed by the moves a piece of fiction or poetry make, but more often than not reading the latest book by an admired writer, even a writer I consider experimental, feels like slipping back into an old, comfortable shirt. Rarely does a writer push against themselves in unexpected ways. But you do see it: after the maximalist *Underworld* (1997), DeLillo's slender, stripped-down *The Body Artist* (2001) was unexpected—and interesting partly because of that. After his massive single paragraph novels, Thomas Bernhard's collection of short-shorts, *The Voice Imitator* (1977), feels shocking. But are they as experimental when considered in the light of what DeLillo and Bernhard wrote after, or only at the particular historical moment of their appearance?

***

I've several times made the mistake of trying to explain to students why, back when I was an undergraduate, the more minimalist stories of Raymond Carver seemed "experimental." Today, this baffles them. In his first two books, Carver (with Gordon Lish's help) was writing in a way that was different than what we'd seen: stripped down stories, abrupt endings, little interior space: different fictional gestures than we were accustomed to. The reason such stories were taught in writing workshops in the 1980s was because they felt different and new. But very quickly, as other writers and students of writing imitated them, they began to feel less experimental and more foundational for the fiction that followed.

***

I've had a similar experience with George Saunders' fiction. I taught *Civilwarland in Bad Decline* (1996) at Oklahoma State University in 1996, just a few months after that book came out. Students loved it: it felt to them (and to me) slightly but genuinely distinct from anything else they had read. Eight or nine years later, I taught it again, expecting students to love it just as much, but was surprised to find some of them indifferent to the book. "I don't know," said one shrugging student when I asked why, "it reminded me too much of other things I've read." When I pressed him about what those other things were, he named writers who had started publishing after Saunders, all of whom had acknowledged his influence or even been blurbed by him.

Certain experiments fall victim to their own success. They reorient the literary field in such a way that they no longer feel as experimental or original as they initially did, largely because they were so influential, and so other writers changed the way they wrote because of them. If an experiment is a success, it shifts literary culture and hides how innovative that gesture originally felt.

It's hard for us to imagine linear perspective was ever an experiment because it has become so pervasive. It is hard to imagine that there was a time when clues were not a crucial part of the detective story, since they have become pervasive and essential to detective fiction since. In writing, so many things began as experiments but, over time, have come to seem a standard part of a writer's bag of tools. It's easy to forget they weren't always thought of in this way, that they weren't even noticed until someone experimented with them.

***

The reverse can also happen. I've sometimes taught a book and have been surprised by how startled the students are by its gestures, by how radical they find it. Ann Quin's *Berg* (1964), for instance, which by now is one of my favorite old shirts: the thorniness of the language, the way interior and exterior shift without notice, the associative progression, the performative qualities of the prose, are difficult for them in a way that I can, if I think back far enough, remember they once were for me. "Oh right," I have to remind myself, "this is unlike anything you've ever seen." Something is going on in their head that's no longer going on in mine: they are reading a book that causes them to reorient their sense of the literary field, that opens up possibilities for them. But that reorientation already happened for me back when I first read Quin. I'm the writer I am because it happened.

"Experimental writing," Warren Motte suggests, "obliges us to read experimentally." But this isn't a constant. What feels like experimental reading at first go becomes simply a developed strategy of reading on a second read. Very quickly books become territorialized by a reader, paths becoming more and more mentally engrained with each re-reading. If I'm re-reading Joyce's *Ulysses* (1922) after having had two grad classes on the book and having read it on my own several times, I lug a whole apparatus along with me. I can no longer read that book, only re-read it, but the same is true of most books I read more than once.

***

To be an experimental writer demands a kind of insistence on continued curiosity of approach, a willingness to keep shifting the ground on which you stand, an attempt to let go of as much of your baggage as you can. The moment you become comfortable should be the moment you are compelled to try something else. So much of what gets called "experimental" consists of a writer repeating the same riffs he (usually this sort of writer is male) has been doing from the beginning or, worse, imitating the style of writers who came before. If we take the term experimental seriously, I'd argue, there are genuinely experimental gestures, located historically and in relation to the rest of a writer's work, and then there are gestures that remake or rework experiments done better by others. As a writer, you have to ask yourself: are you experimenting in a way that genuinely tries to explore new territory or are you the equivalent of a high school chemistry class rotely following a textbook to reproduce a carefully vetted (and thus safe) "experiment"?

***

For me, right now, one of the places where the most interesting experiments are occurring are at the intersections between genres, with work interested in crossing genre barriers or blurring genre distinctions. On the one hand, such work can blur the line between fiction, poetry and prose; on the other it can have one foot in so-called popular genres and the other in literary fiction. Both types experiment with using the ideas and techniques of one thing to energize another, believing that a kind of short-circuiting of ideas we have about what genre can do might lead to new sorts of writing happening. Such writers give themselves permission to disrupt established divisions, to break things, to take chances. They do this gambling that the results can be illuminating.

At the same time, I wonder how long such gestures will still feel experimental. By the time something is recognized as experimental, it is already on its way to becoming anything but. Work combining elements of both literary fiction and genre fiction is more and more widely accepted: at some point, it becomes a norm and a model rather than an experiment. Similarly, hybrid and blurred genre work acts more and more like a genre, as if the writers have agreed to the same "rules."

***

And yet, there are always places to go—we just have to be, as writers, of a mindset to keep moving, to take risks, to experiment without keeping one eye focused on our literary reputation or our fame. Take for instance Damien Ober, whose *Doctor Benjamin Franklin's Dream America* (2014) takes 1777 America and overlays it with internet technology, aliens, sea monsters, witches and general madness. The result is a unique experiment, one that says more about what America is and what it has become than a strictly historical novel could. Or Kathryn Davis's brilliant *Duplex* (2013), which seems like a piece of realistic fiction about the 1950s until the moment when we realize this world contains, without explanation, sorcerers and robots and even stranger things. Or Robert Kloss's *The Woman Who Lived Amongst the Cannibals* (2017), which takes a historical captivity narrative and energizes it by exchanging sentences for brief, startling phrases separated by dashes. All three of these bring to the "historical" something quite different than what we expect, through historical cross-pollination, through fantasy, through disruptions of syntax. You might see precursors for all three in the work of Robert Coover or John Fowles or Angela Carter, or even the "Patterns of Force" Star Trek episode, but even knowing those precursors, they remain surprising, original, and exciting.

But, of course, the fact that there are three quite different writers working on the borders of the historical to create something distinct suggests that this particular experiment is already beginning to cohere into something definitive, something that future writers—including myself—can pay attention to, torque, and build on. By the time you notice a trend beginning to cohere, experiments are perhaps beginning to move elsewhere.

***

As writers interested in experiment, we strive to be aware of the literary past without feeling beholden to it—but aware enough not to repeat it, and perceptive enough to see those moments of eddy and divagation in literary history which might lead our thinking elsewhere, which might lead us to new experiments, a few of which will be, hopefully, successful.

12

The Literature of Extinction
Douglas Glover

1. Nostalgia (the Death of God)

In his essay "The Depreciated Legacy of Cervantes," Milan Kundera offers a poignant confession of allegiance to an outmoded Humanism and an aesthetic of lightness and play, which, at the outset of the Modern Era, already suggested every human possibility except, perhaps, the possibility that we might cease to be. I say outmoded, but Kundera himself recognizes that the world he inhabits is alien to the human project. He calls it the time of terminal paradoxes, a time conditioned by the unifying, simplifying engines of mass media (which, in his mind, are against the complexity of novels). The era we are talking of contains the birth and death of the individual, the death of God, everything from Pico della Mirandola's "Oration on the Dignity of Man" to the smoking furnaces of Bergen-Belsen.

But first there is a bloom, a divine afflatus. Rabelais invents the proto-novel out of the Menippean satire (from the Latin *satura*, a stuffed sausage, or a hodge-podge), which we might think of as the earliest outbreak of experimental literature. Menippus's work is now lost but, by repute, was characterized by irony, quotation, hybrid form, parody, and bawdy humour. Shortly after Rabelais, Cervantes writes a novel about a man rendered insane by books. A decade later, in 1615, he publishes a sequel, in which the hero has to deal with characters who have read the first book. An imitator (what we might today call a troll) is wandering around Spain calling himself Don Quixote. This causes Don Quixote such anxiety that he begs the local mayor to certify his authenticity as the real Don Quixote. *Don Quixote* is about the anxiety of a character dimly aware that he is trapped inside a book. In other words, Cervantes is already conscious of the bookishness of books and the games that can be played with words and the artifice of verisimilitude.

A hundred and fifty years later Laurence Sterne composes a novel without a plot, the blank page, the black page, and a book with plot diagrams. After Menippus, Rabelais, Cervantes, and Sterne, there are no more techniques of experiment to be invented; they are only reinvented with different explanations. But the novel itself takes a detour into what Kundera calls the realistic imperative. Novelistic experiment resurfaces in Central Europe with the advent of various modernisms (with Schlegel's German Romanticism in the background, hence Kundera's love of irony and complexity) in the work of Broch and Musil and later the Polish experimentalist Witold Gombrowicz (whose novel *Cosmos* [1965] subtly echoes *Don Quixote*; it's about a character trapped in an image pattern). Kundera has, here, grasped a thread of experiment, of playfulness, that is also against the decline of values, the loss of Being, and the entropic tendency of modernity, which seeks only homogeneity and profit. (Cervantes is brilliant on the cruel and air-headed free spirits of the kleptocratic late capitalism *avant la lettre*.)

2. Cynicism (Lifting the Veil)

What we more commonly call experimental literature, what we might now, in the twenty-first century, call Establishment experimentalism, arises in the late nineteenth century (for art, with the Impressionists) and the early twentieth century (for literature, with the Surrealists). It evolves as an outsider (Salon des Refusés, 1863) critique of a basket of Renaissance and Enlightenment assumptions about truth, reason, language, self, and God. It lifts the veil (as in *The Wizard of Oz* [1939]) on the comforting and Philistine illusions of the modern Humanist project.

The work is difficult because it's new, but not so new that it can't be understood with the help of a little theory from Nietzsche and Darwin, of course. But Ferdinand de Saussure's analysis of the structure of the linguistic sign accelerates much of the avant-garde invention by separating the sign from the signified, gesture from meaning. Much twentieth century experimental art is based on the inversion of sign/signified priority. The American experimental novelist John Hawkes puts it succinctly when he says that plot, character, setting and theme (conventional devices promoting the illusion of verisimilitude) are the enemies of the novel, while repeated image and repeated event are the true essence of literary prose. If there is no signified (meaning), then pattern, brute sound (sound poetry), dream (Surrealism), and the accidental and the ready-made (Duchamp) become acceptable avenues of art.

The author ceases to exist conceptually. So does the reader. Words float. As reality comes into question, so does the illusion of reality as in literary realism and the techniques of verisimilitude. The emperor has no clothes. The veil must be lifted. This is an oddly Platonic critique of literary arts. In the *Republic* (c. 380 BCE), Plato argues against poets because their words might, through the action of the imagination, lead readers to think something is true that is not (Plato did not much trust the intelligence of the common person).

This austere modernity, modernity-from-the-outside, separates itself from the consumer art of the nineteenth and twentieth centuries and becomes a High Art and a minority art. This new Establishment experimental art reaches its apotheosis in 2011 when Kenneth Goldsmith (a professional academician) reads Brooklyn radio traffic reports at the White House as poetry. Now, found poems and erasure poetry are all the craze at the creative writing programs. Oulipo is the new, cool (old) thing. The rebellion of the rejects that began as a flank attack on the school art of early bourgeois capitalism has been coopted by late capitalism minus the human element.

3. The Return of the Repressed, or the Aesthetics of Extinction

History is a tide of concurrent stories that break over the present like waves (some people still think they are living this history or that history, and the discourses persist in a zombie state).

The old styles of experiment all persist today in varying degrees of vitality. The new experimentalism, the newest loosely gathered basket of foundational concepts, foresees a moment when this will all be washed away with the extinction of the race (now imminent; some say it has already happened). The new aesthetics flow from this moment.

We see the world more clearly now (we think). It's very small, dirty, crowded with people, and heating up. The Anthropocene is the new name given to the period of time (roughly beginning with the Neolithic) human beings have had a significant impact on the environment. Now we know there is no free lunch, and the hubris of our assumption that the earth was an infinite, free resource specially catered for us by the gods is beginning to look like a monumental gaffe.

Nor are we essentially different from the other orders of being (say, trees, rocks, newts); consciousness may be a neural anomaly, or, as the A. I. researchers like to say, an emergent property, that is, a side effect of our neural interaction with whatever we are interacting with (just as the colour of an object is not a property of the object but a side effect of the wavelengths of light interacting with eye neurons). Not a self, a soul, a ghost in the machine, but a wisp of smoke, dream-like and temporary.

The new aesthetics, like the old aesthetics, have something to do with what we think reality is and how we might represent that in art. And as the Spanish novelist Germán Sierra suggests (in a remarkable essay called "Deep Media Fiction"), a good deal of what seems new is repackaged nostalgia for the human; we invent zombie fiction and sci-fi movies in which corpses or androids develop a soul, often better than the humans they deal with (we are saved, in a sense, by passing along our humanity). But if what is real is something like waves and particles interacting in peculiar ways and consciousness is a byproduct, if as the philosopher (of the post-Anthropocene) Claire Colebrook suggests, everything tends towards "indifference" (which I take to be undifferentiated, chaotic, unconscious being), then any sort of writing must engage with its own impossibility.

Any traditional form only reproduces the Humanist myth; a formless book risks failure (unreadability). Reading Sierra's essay,

I am reminded of Heidegger's effort to invent a philosophical language to describe Being. Language itself is a construct of consciousness, which is an emergent property and not a thing. We are talking about using a figment squared to describe something we cannot know. And so the new experimental writing falls back on the age-old devices of allegory, constructed chaos, and suggestive reference.

The operative word here is "suggestive"; the new literature is suggestive of a reality that cannot be described or even approached. Echoing Heidegger's obscurity on the subject Being, Sierra writes in his essay that the new literature attempts "to get different portions of reality to emit vibrations that might (or might not) have any observable effect." It borrows, as constructive analogies, words like the uncanny from Freud and schizophrenia and deterritorialization from Deleuze and Guattari. It borrows from cybernetics and computer programming (somehow I think this is an appropriation that lends an eery, inhuman tenor to the writing as well as a pseudo-scientific authority) and it borrows from pop culture, horror movies, and science fiction (Lovecraft is an avatar).

The spate of dystopian books and movies of the last couple of decades are forerunners, always projecting a survival of something recognizably human. But the new experimental literature is using a human artefact, language, to imagine the post-human *without survival*. I am speaking here of Ccru Writing, work out of and inspired by the fabled Cybernetic Culture Research Unit at the University of Warwick, most notably Reza Negarestani's 2008 novel *Cyclonopedia: Complicity with Anonymous Materials*, a horrific Pynchonesque extravaganza about oil, the War on Terror, terror, and archaeology. "The Middle East is a sentient entity—it is alive!"

Terror is the dominant tone of the post-human, of End Times. How could we expect the inhuman to be anything but inhuman? In America, Bret Easton Ellis's fingerprints are everywhere. I am thinking especially of the serial killer in Blake Butler's *300,000,000* (2014) or the cyber-rhapsody of rape in Jan Ramjerdi's *RE>LA>VIR* (2000). "We are connected now. Basically I rape her in the ass with the barrel of my gun, handle shoved up my own cunt so I can come too." All in the form of a computer print-out.

Call such books disturbances in a field. Beauty, after all, is only a comforting Humanist illusion. Every time there is a revolution in our concept of reality, there is a fresh outburst of experiment in the arts, fresh disturbances in the field. The newest experiments embrace the entropic tendency of late modernity; they seek to vibrate in sympathy with the fundamental indifference of things. The project is paradoxical (even comical), sending a message—THE END IS NEAR—while trying to engage an audience. There is no message and there is no audience— soon(ish).

13
Poetry is Not Public Policy
Kenneth Goldsmith

Poetry is not public policy. Poetry has neither a public nor a policy. Poetry's power is its powerlessness, which is the power to imagine the unimaginable. Poetry's inability to change anything is its ability, it's disability its acuity. Poetry's inversion of logic is its logic, its stasis it's movement, its impoverishment its wealth. The only thing realizable about poetry is its unrealizability which, freed of pragmatics, makes it completely realizable. Its low bar— a zero bar—is its democracy. A worthless commodity, poetry is free to all. We're giving away rocks today. Everyone can have as many as they want. Poetry thrives on speculation, proposition its fulfillment. In this way, poetry is completely conceptual; I think it, it exists. No permission needed. Ask no one. No gatekeepers necessary because there's nothing there to protect, it's all there for the taking. In this way, poetry is completely romantic; I dream it, it exists. In this way dreaming is democratic. Everyone dreams and everyone dreams at no cost. In this way, there is nothing elitist about dreaming. My nightly dreams are no better than yours. My nightly dreams are worth no more than yours. My dreams are no more causal than yours. My nightly dreams are as unrealizable as yours. They're dreams, after all; they mean a lot to you and to me, but mean little to anyone else. Who cares? Would you forego dreaming?

'Pataphysics is foundational to poetry. The science of imaginary solutions to imaginary problems is definitive. Your problems are imaginary; so are your solutions. Give it up. Let it go. In this way, let the illogic become logical. Illogic as resistance.

Dissolve binaries, live in the gray zone. As an inversion, functionless becomes functional, radical, changeable. But 'pataphysics is a bad way to conduct social justice. In the real world, real solutions are required for real problems. This is not poetry's work. Poetry's work is to jam systems with irrationality, with illogic and abstraction. This is where it works best. Take to the streets, yell at the top of your lungs for change. You will make a difference. But don't put that burden on poetry, for poetry is reverse engineered for self-destruction. Bombs will explode. But nobody will get hurt.

Mistaking poetry for politics is a result of a malfunctioning spellcheck. Poetry's ethics is aethics: malleable, soft, playful and speculative. Actually, let's imagine a world without ethics. Let's rob empty banks for the joy of theft. Theft without consequence. Compassionate anarchy. We've got water pistols. Hands up! This is a robbery! We're striking Jeffersonian candles. Please, take my flame. Poets are speculators of empty markets, trading Monopoly money. Mistaking Monopoly wealth for actual wealth is like mistaking poetry for public policy. We're all wealthy. Our banks are brimming with Monopoly credit.

Appropriation has three definitions: monetary appropriation, aesthetic appropriation, and straight up theft. Draw from the common bank account, empty and therefore symbolic. No animals were harmed in the making of this movie. Try not to mistake your poetic metaphors for reality. There's no violence in cutting text, dear—it is merely a function, a keystroke, a piece of programming. Cutting text is in no way like cutting flesh. If you don't believe me, cut some text, then take a sharp razor to your arm. You'll see that they have nothing to do with one another. Poetic imagination as is commonly learned is a mistake, confounding differences so obvious that they would not be mistaken by a child. This is why I am opposed to poetic imagination.

Poetry makes nothing happen, which makes it perverse and propulsive. There are many ills in the world; poetry is not one of them. There are many things worth battling for in the world; poetry is not one of them. There are many battles where there is actually something to be won; poetry is not one of them. Thankfully.

Recuse yourself. When you wage poetic war you are truly fighting windmills. Even if you conceive of poetry as a symbolic battleground, corrupted by shady institutional systems, look hard at what's at stake. You'll find the glass is fully empty, which is exactly where it's always been and always will be.

Heroin also makes nothing happen. It takes people and renders them into object lessons, echoing Man Ray's alleged provocation "take something useful and make it useless." But back up the camera and you'll see that heroin, in fact, is rather productive. It's a lucrative business, tied to organized crime and cartels. In fact, heroin makes a lot happen by integrating itself seamlessly to capitalism and globalism. Poetry, on the other hand, has no such problem. It is neither capitalist or global. Yet it does destroy lives as a result of attrition ironically drawing poets into the ecosystem of capitalism and globalism as they become addicted to narcotics and alcohol, unwillingly colliding the useful with the useless. In this way, poetry abets criminality and churns gold—but not for poets, alas.

The world is voracious for copies of just about everything — except poetry. I have the most innovative idea for a book of poems, which I post on the internet to entice readers. Not only do readers not come, but the Chinese bootleggers don't bother either. No one wants poetry. You can't give it away. Charles Bernstein has commented that a piece of paper with a poem printed on it devalues that piece of paper. A blank piece of a paper is worth more than a poem; a blank piece of paper can be used to write a love letter, or an invoice, a menu—all things useful and necessary. Poetry is useless and unnecessary. When the rest of the world is worried about having their ideas stolen, poets have no such fears.

Sometimes, inventors go to the trouble of making something artisanal that can't be duplicated. By going backwards, the world moves forward. Yet no matter what move poetry makes, it remains stuck where it is. In the fast world of globalized hypercapitalism, poetry is simply not allowed to participate. Poets continue to make marble iPhone cases, as they have since Homer. We are useless. And it's a privilege.

You might say I'm naïve. Naïveté is a symptom of innocence. By daring to be naïve, one can become newly innocent.

Once-innocents or lapsed-innocents can salvage that state merely by granting themselves the permission to do so. Paradise regained is no small task. To even contemplate it is daunting. One must renounce the accumulation of a lifetime's worth of knowledge—even if it's faulty knowledge—which for many is the equivalent of self-abnegation, erasure, deletion, and voluntary bankruptcy. Buckminster Fuller did exactly that. Having taken a conventional path in a business based on innovation, he failed. On the verge of suicide, he had an instantaneous realization that, to quote the Firesign Theatre, everything you know is wrong. At the moment he dared to be naïve, and by undertaking a rejection of everything in the world that he himself could not empirically prove, he became an inventor Back to square one, he had no choice but start inventing from scratch.

In 1964 Jasper Johns wrote, "Take an object. Do something to it. Do something else to it." What it is we are supposed to do with it is not specified. Instead, the act of doing in and of itself is sufficiently transformative. What happens to the object might be irrelevant in comparison to what happens to us by transforming it. A simple recipe, Johns' edict is a call to action without the anticipation of results, running in place, treading water, an active stasis. A variant of Johns: "Take something useful and make it useless." Uselessness is the province of art. Man Ray perfectly demonstrated this with his 1958 readymade Gift, which famously consists of a flat iron with fourteen thumbtacks attached to its bottom surface, as did Méret Oppenheim with her fur teacup. Both sculptures are useless objects that have unintentionally become useful as iconic demonstrations of uselessness.

W. H. Auden said, "Poetry makes nothing happen," and that nothing is at the heart of its potent resistance. The idea of making nothing happen is perverse in a world bent on results. But then again, the act of making art is perverse for the same reasons. The twisting of language, using it in ways that deviate from the norm, contrary to accepted standards, is also perverse. Common sense would steer us away from such aberrance: Isn't it difficult enough to understand one another with the language we have already? Why make it worse? The poet is often speaking the language of one, and because of that language's limited reach its audience is either circumscribed or the poet speaks only to herself. It is for this reason that poetry is both so reviled and ignored. Refusing to partake in exchange and commerce, poetry is dismissed as being "unproductive" in every way imaginable. (The worst words a parent could ever hear from a child is that they have chosen to be a poet.)

The solitariness of the poet is embodied perversity: onanistic, self-contained, and nongenerative. It closely resembles certain forms of sexual perversion in its singularity, isolation, and relative ineffectiveness. Flashing or streaking is like poetry, temporal occurrences that half-wish to provoke, but are too ashamed and cowardly to commit a crime more severe than a misdemeanor. The poet's antiheroics ride a line between shame and desire. I read a poem, I briefly lift my skirt to show my genitals. I submit a poem, I momentarily display my breasts with an up-and-down lifting of my shirt and/or bra. I write a poem, I quickly display my bare buttocks by pulling down my trousers and underwear. I tweet a poem, I fleetingly run naked thorough a public place. Look at me. Please don't look at me. The effect of either the poetic or the mildly sexual action is affective, a double-edged blade that cuts me more than it does you. If poetry could change anything, they'd make it illegal. Instead poetry is a series of vague refusals that cancel each other out: I would prefer not to. But I would prefer to. Active abstention. Substantive blanks. Propulsive contradiction. Hyperactive stasis. Poetry and perversion both express a mild disapproval that never rises to the level of active opposition.

Be realistic, demand the impossible. The enemy of movement is skepticism. Everything that has been realized comes from dynamism, which comes from spontaneity. Forget everything you've been taught. Start by dreaming. This concerns everyone. When people notice they are bored, they stop being bored. Chance must be systematically explored. Forget everything you've been taught. Start by dreaming. When examined, answer with questions. No forbidding allowed. Imaginary solutions to imaginary problems. There is no solution because there is no problem.

poetry as a safe space for imagining solutions to problems
poetry can't change anything because it isn't meant to
poetry is expression, not an action

14

Hello Stranger
Laird Hunt

"Brakhage Meets Tarkovsky (as told to Jenny Dorn)" sheds light on an extraordinary encounter that took place on the fringes of the 1983 Telluride Film Festival. In it, Stan Brakhage describes showing his films to Andrei Tarkovsky in a tiny (6 by 10) hotel room and the explosively negative reaction he received to *Window Water Baby Moving, Dog Star Man, Part IV, Untitled No. 6, Made Manifest* and others. The scene is crazy: the films are projected right onto faded hotel wallpaper; there are eight hot bodies in the room; Tarkovsky keeps going ballistic in Russian, and his translator hands over the substance of what he is saying to Brakhage, whose heart is "absolutely breaking for the films." Brakhage defends them nonetheless. Here's a taste of the exchange:

"What is this? It doesn't mean anything, it's just capricious." And I'm coming back and saying, "Shut up and look and you'll see there's a melodic line and shapes don't just occur anywhere in the frame, there's a balance." "But what does it mean?" "What do you mean what does it mean? You have a lot of statements about music in your films..." "But this isn't the same as music," and it goes on and on.

Indeed it does, although the séance finally ends in a tedious fizzle when a very bad film (something Brakhage and Tarkovsky can agree on) by an unnamed Russian émigré is screened. Fortunately, there is an epilogue to the story. Zbigniew Rybczynski, the Polish animator who was one of the 8 in the room, catches up with Brakhage the next day and, after haranguing him about the irrelevance of art, brushes aside Brakhage's disclaimers about the poor viewing conditions for his films (shown on wallpaper, no one would shut up, etc.) with the following:

> "Don't you know that Tarkovsky went on talking about this for the rest of the day? For two hours they were raging and carrying on. And he's still talking about it!" He said he'd known Tarkovsky for years on and off in Poland, and many people think he's taken a vow of silence like in Andrei Rublev. For weeks he'll never say a word. He said he'd never heard him talk so much all at once and he said, "I'm very jealous!" He said he'd never seen him so excited about anything and that my films would cast a shadow through his work.

Tarkovsky only had three years left to live, so the question of whether or not any real Brakhagian shadow was paid forward is debatable. Still, it was in reading that last bit that I felt the deeper pull of something like recognition. Because without ever quite so articulating it, and allowing for multiple imperfections in the analogy, I have been laboring in my work for many years to write like those two men made their films. Or rather, to experiment in my writing the way (or—to shave it down even further—in *some* of the ways) those two men experimented in their films.

A couple of examples might help make clear what I'm getting at. *Mothlight* (1963) by Brakhage is a little over three minutes of insect wings and plant shards, which Brakhage collected, pressed between pieces of tape and fed through a film printer. On the one hand it's a mini visual essay on light, time, material and method of production; on the other, it's an exploration of mortality, grief, rage and beauty, echoing and pre-echoing Virginia Woolf's "The Death of the Moth" and W. G. Sebald's *Austerlitz* (2001). *Stalker* (1979), by Tarkovsky, is 160 minutes longer than *Mothlight*, incorporates scenes, characters and narrative, actually uses a camera, and relies, as does so much of Tarkovsky's work, on incredibly long shots. On the one hand, it's a narrative investigation of humanist wreckage in a post-nuclear nightmare; on the other, it's an exploration of mortality, grief, rage and beauty, which echoes Europe's battlefields and evokes deeply othered spaces like the one depicted in Samuel R. Delany's great *Dhalgren* (1975).

Certainly, we infer our own rhizomes, manipulate their terms and this is all, no doubt, rigged from the start. Brakhage? Tarkovsky? Come on! Still, there it is, and somewhere in there, I work. What does this mean or what has it meant for my writing? Not necessarily the tantalizing fruits of a blurring of beautiful, strange, sinuous, surprising narratives (Tarkovsky) and beautiful, strange, gorgeously gapped surprising non-narratives (Brakhage): instead I find that what I have done rolls along entirely different sets of rail or, better, sits side by side though not symmetrically in the same room. On one side, there are the city novels, *The Impossibly* (2001), *The Exquisite* (2006), and *Ray of the Star* (2009), along with all my early attempts at writing unreasonably compressed stories that, with all time beaten out of them, turned out as prose poetry; on the other, there are the rural and history focused novels, *Indiana, Indiana* (2003), *Kind One* (2012), *Neverhome* (2014), and *The Evening Road* (2017). The former bunching finds me working heavily with digression and recursiveness, attempting to deconstruct narrative and explode time, flicking my language-lensed super eight around in urban forests and never letting it linger too long. The latter has its lens pointed fixedly at the past: whole heavy cuts of story come out of those verbal longs takes, out of this extended appraisal, out of forgetting for extended periods to blink.

So, yes, I look back at the novels I have written and see them sitting in a small room fizzing back and forth at each other, speaking slightly and even completely different languages. But they are in a room together. They are together. At least in me.

I am thinking aloud and being aspirational here.

Just as I am thinking aloud and being aspirational when I introduce another exhibit into the conversation—one that plants its flag both closer (it's a book) and farther (it was published in 1923) away from my aesthetic base camp: *Cane* by Jean Toomer. *Cane*, a slender work composed of poems, song fragments, sketches, visual symbols, theatrical interventions and stories—is its own snug space amped up to radioactive levels by a radically different approach.

Maybe, if I were to make a fiction out of the Brakhage/Tarkosky encounter, I would place a copy of *Cane* on a little table by the only bed. Every now and again, perhaps at a reel change, Rybczynski might pick it up and start to open it only, when the fireworks get going again, to put it back down. *Cane's* pieces are set in the North—where Toomer was from—as well as in the South—where he briefly spent time. The northern pieces hum and buzz with urban energy enveloped by regret; the southern pieces, small town or rural, bow under enormous weight, are governed by impossible hope and sharp, sweet rage. They are doing different work and behave accordingly, and Toomer put them all into one book. He let the whole hiss and rattle, sing and moan. It's a thing of great power and beauty achieved not only by the frictive discreteness of its many pieces but also by the many bridges built across its gaps. In one of the stories, a woman sitting in a theater in the North sends roots down through the floor that travel all the way back down South. And so we see, vividly, how the one thing is linked to the other, that it cannot *be* without the other. This does not make them the same.

Nor are my novels—despite all the bridges that could be easily argued into existence between them—the same. In this context, and considering the different nodes of power I have been pulled toward over the years and the ways in which my books are attracted to and repulsed by each other just as I have been attracted to and repulsed by the artists whose work I've loved (let's throw in here the output of Max Richter, Louise Bourgeoise, James Agee, Gabriel Orozco, László Krasznahorkai, Philip K. Dick, Svetlana Alexievich and Marie NDiaye) I might argue, just for this moment, something like the opposite of this wonderful shard from Warren Motte's *Mirror Gazing* (2014). "'Nobody likes to recognize himself as a stranger,' argues Maurice Blanchot, 'in a mirror where he doesn't see his double but instead someone he would have liked to be' (*Michel Foucault tel que je l'imagine* [1986])." For even as I'm drawn, mothlike, to exemplary, idiosyncratic, high-octane artistic instance, I breathe a sigh of existential relief on behalf of my writing when I realize again and again that someone I would have liked to be *is not me*. It means I get to keep attempting, exactly, to be in my work, to the extent possible, what others whose work thrills me are not.

I may in the end be left with nothing. But it will be my own nothing: rich, maybe; *Cane* class, doubt it; varied, certainly; radioactive, we'll see.

15
The Addressed Poem of the Day
Jacques Jouet

Translated by Ian Monk

Since 1ˢᵗ April 1992, I have been composing *poems of the day*, a dated, localized poem, freshly produced each day. After a good twenty years, they are legion.

The first four years were published in 1999 by P. O. L as *Navet, linge, œil-de-vieux*. The next four years, *Du jour*, came out from the same publishers in November 2013.

Over the years, various procedures have been adopted: series of still lifes, portrait-poems, addressed poems, poems while listening to music…On 29ᵗʰ May 2013, I started what will be the final—and unfinishable—procedure in this enterprise, *the addressed poem of the day*.

The idea of the *addressed poem of the day* is to appeal to as many people as possible, one by one.

What hope can a poet writing today have that seven billion human beings will read his pathetic little poems, as if he were a Baudelaire? But another hope might be that all human beings, all of our fellows, common candidates, unknown friends, brothers…will one day have their own poem, written first and foremost for them.

This is why I started by picking up the directory of telephone subscribers in the French *département* of l'Ain (01). They are listed by town. The first one, L'Abergement-Clémenciat, the second one, L'Abergement-de-Varey, and so on. To each and every subscriber, I am sending, by post, a poem. With it, I enclose my address and a brief description of the overall project. It remains to be seen if, in my lifetime, I get to l'Aisne, and then, after France, to Gabon, and after Gabon, to Greece, and so on up to Zimbabwe before starting again with South Africa (*Afrique du Sud*), with Finland to finish. This might be termed transcendence, in the only form of it that I recognize: the one deriving from very large numbers. It's unreasonable. So what? At least I'll have tried. Who knows? I may get some help from other people during my lifetime; then maybe they'll continue after my death. That makes for a lot of "mays."

So as not to fall into the fatal monotony of a single list, nothing will prevent me, given the right circumstances, from anticipating by covering other fragments of particular territories or groups, thanks to indications from various "pathfinders."

*

Ain

As of 1ˢᵗ October 2013, Jean-Paul Honoré has joined the project by going through the directory of l'Ain (01) backwards: its final town is called Vonnas. We will meet up, some time soon, in the middle of the list. This will occur in the town of Jassans-Riottier.

L'Ételon

On 16ᵗʰ, 17ᵗʰ and 18ᵗʰ November 2013, Patrick Biau, Gérald Castéras, Jean-Paul Honoré, and Cécile Riou and I addressed a poem to all of the inhabitants of the village L'Ételon (03360).

Bourges

As writer in residence in Bourges (2014-2015, with the association *les mille univers*), I addressed over a thousand poems to the inhabitants of that town, with the help of my poet friends and the participants in the workshops I led. (In particular I acknowledge Patrick Biau, Valérie Lotti and Annie Pellet, who were especially productive…) (This series of poems is due to be published by *les mille univers*.)

Valvins

In 2015, at the Stéphane Mallarmé Museum in Valvins, Vulaines-sur-Seine in the Seine-et-Marne (77), a group of poets consisting of Benoît Casas, Frédéric Forte, Jean-Paul Honoré, Cécile Riou and I sent six hundred addressed poems to the local inhabitants.

Århus
In April 2015, in Århus, Denmark, I composed a hundred and one addressed poems in situ, translated into Danish by Steen Bille Jørgensen. (This series of poems is due to be published in a bilingual edition in Denmark.)

Victoria
In Victoria BC, Canada, in July 2015, a hundred and ten addressed poems were composed by a group of poets made up of Marc Lapprand, Natali Leduc, Cécile Riou and myself. Following Natali Leduc's suggestion, the common point about the poems in this series is that they mingle the French and English languages on each page.

Limerick
On the 16th and 17th October 2015, at the University of Limerick, Ireland, I addressed twenty-nine poems to the twenty-nine participants at the "Systems" symposium organized by ADEFFI (*Association des études françaises et francophones d'Irlande*). These poems were composed while listening to the contributions. (This series of poems was published online in the *The Irish Journal of French Studies,* vol. 15, 2015.)

Vert-Saint-Denis
In January/March 2016. Jean-Paul Honoré, then writer in residence at Vert-Saint-Denis in the Seine-et-Marne, invited Benoît Casas, Jacques Jouet, Cécile Riou and Jacques Roubaud to join him in the composition and addressing of poems to the approximately four hundred members of the Jean Vilar municipal library. These poems are on the subject of Japan or, more generally, travel.

Lozère
As of 1st February 2016, Cécile Riou has joined the project, taking the directory of the Lozère (48) from its beginning. Its first town is Albaret-le-Comtal.

—to be continued—

*

As an example, here is the first series of these poems, written for l'Ain, chronologically.

Each addressed poem is printed out, then sent by post, with this text at the bottom of the page:

The idea of the addressed poem of the day is to appeal to as many people as possible, one by one.

What hope can a poet writing today have that seven billion human beings will read his pathetic little poems, as if he were a Baudelaire? But another hope might be that all human beings will one day have their own poem, written first and foremost for them.

This is why I started by picking up the directory of telephone subscribers in the French département of l'Ain (01). So what? At least I'll have tried. And then, who knows? I may get some help from other people.

Jacques Jouet—41, rue Popincourt, 75011 Paris

29th May 2013, Paris
(poem addressed to **Gabriel Alzingre**)

The postman has wings, in a Pasolini film,
for good etymological reasons.

A poem has words, in any case,
the first in a series.

This stamp is still red from Marianne's kiss
but for how much longer?

Men's ideas, on boulevard Richard-Lenoir,
are sometimes rich and sometimes dark.

Once things have been said
food has already become advanced.

30th May 2013, Paris
(poem addressed to **Nathalie Arenas**)

You count seven grains of sand
too few for a fight
not making a beach
nor a bed for romping
or for turbots on a slab
for the Queen of Sheba
not even stinging the Devil's eyes.

31 May 2013, Blois
(poem addressed to **Alain Argentero**)

I was in Blois, where I saw the bridge
Jacques-Gabriel, named after its architect.
The roadway rises then descends again
at a very obtuse angle
amid the ford of the wide, high Loire.
Very elegant, this angel's wing
if a bridge is an angel's wing
as a Serb legend states, so as to forget the
    devil's claw:
the symmetrical arches, of increasing then
    decreasing size
and the central pivot forming its peak.
Upstream, protecting the piles from the
    current's force, are "fore-beaks,"
as cantilevers are called in French, and as
    these ducks know.
The stronger you are, the more clement you
    can be
and the more effectively
you protect yourself.

1ˢᵗ June 2013, Paris
(poem addressed to **Raphaël Badot**)

A tree, apparently, is not a tree-individual
but a group, a society
and if death is not part of its program

we can speak, in its case,
of long longevity with good reason.

It should thus be here
that metempsychosis takes root
Philemon the oak and Baucis the lime-ess
multiplying in two colonies

which would mingle their branches
in memory of having been welcoming.

(poem addressed to **Sylvain Balandras**)

You do nothing, says Gilles, and still the
    forest
puts itself back together, there, at your feet.
A return of the primordial wood for you
wishing your eyes and your attention well.

On a blank page
on the other hand
you do nothing: no blotches
no traces of footsteps.

2nd June 2013, Paris
(poem addressed to **Fabien Banderier**)

Today is Sunday
and I hear Tintin's voice
in amazement at the moon
still calm this morning
the jam is plum
I empty my intestines
a *Souvenir*? My revenge…

3rd June 2013, Paris
(poem addressed to **Fabrice Barbosa**)
The landscape is homemade, it says so

on the letterbox, I can see it from here
without seeing it, I project myself, casting
  my gaze
I can see nothing, it's nighttime.
I've seen sixty times one thousand landscapes
  at least
but this one I do not know, all the same
it will barely surprise me, except
if I have to take a closer look at it
for some reason or another.
Something in my memory tells me
that at Châtillon-sur-Chalaronne…
that's it, Jesus taught the doctors.

4ᵗʰ June 2013, Paris
(poem addressed to **Rodolphe Baudrand**)

Some street names just aren't possible
for example, Refrigerator
Street, Leg of Lamb Street or
Trash Can, Boulevard or Triple

Twenty Street, *Bible,*
Pork Sausage or Meat & Tater
Street, which would be, at any rate, a
laugh, Streets for a Penalty or Dribble.

No, local politicians are timid
Bodily Hair Street ain't even for the mid
Term. Species of trees in lists

work better, alongside bird
names. No street for the Freshly Interred
none for Tombstones, nor for Masochists.
*
(poem addressed to **Philippe Beaudet**)

It is the triumph of knowledge

which is passing down the avenue
in an elementary school group
with its teacher. Would you
believe it, hush! Must we just shut up
if we want to learn from this shrew
all her wisdom and so recoup
this experience of the nakedly true,
where science is what we acknowledge?

5th June 2013, Poitiers
(poem addressed to **Suzanne Beaudet**)

The oft-taken Paris-Geneva train
traverses the day while bypassing the Dombes
and the train to Limoges the Brenne
and one such other the Sologne …
The ducks know how to make the most of it,
   having no GPS,
or being nothing but.
In turn, a deliveryman enters nonetheless
his profession making him unstoppable
he knows that he's expected
and doesn't drive on the grass.

6th June 2013, Paris
(poem addressed to **Vincent Beaune**, undelivered, returned
to **Marc Lapprand**, the stamp-provider)

I remember once losing it in a town,
well over the top, life just had to change
from start to finish, "come back, come back!"
I was absolutely sure that I wanted to return
or to have returned—I'd lost the word—as a
   revenant.
There is the will of the instant
and the will of commitment
which aren't the same.

It comes down to comparing varied impulses
it's not that it's imprudent
it's more that it's smart. And risky,
this above-named exercise,
which seems alien to the myth of passion.
I can remember
telephoning terribly in a town.
Back then (not that far) it was from a call box.

16

Going Upside-Down: One Poet's Experience with
     Experimental Literature
Julie Larios

When thinking about my approach to "experimental" literature, I decided that reaching for something anecdotal (that is, in the language of some experimental theorists, going for the phenomenal rather than the abstract) would help me. I'm no critic, no theorist. The language of theory leaves me gobsmacked. I can translate it if I work hard at it. In general, translation excites me— I regard the vocabulary, I work on the flow, I look for convergences. But anecdote, not theory, provides my way in to experimental literature, and so I offer this:

The other day, I went into a grocery store looking for food essentials to feed my youngest son (a vegan) and his girlfriend (lactose intolerant.) They were going to be staying with us for a few days, what was in my pantry just wasn't going to do. I'm behind the times; all my entrees touch at least tangentially on meat or cheese. Vegetables, beans, grain, salads—they're what I was taught to plump up a meal with, not to provide the protein. When I say the word "vegan" my mind immediately thinks "tofu" and then thinks "ugh." But this grocery store I was going to is known for organic produce, whole grains, fascinating non-dairy cheese choices, local products—they're a conscientious bunch of people trying to provide alternatives to what many people think of as run-of-the-mill American food excesses like mine.

And since they have a huge building but a small inventory, they rent out space to a video store called Film is Truth (the name lifted from a famous Jean-Luc Godard quotation, "Photography is truth. And film is truth at 24 frames per second") and to a used bookstore called Mt. Baker Books (its name lifted from the mountain to our east.) I skipped the videos—no desire to watch a video while my son and his girlfriend were in town. But on my way out of the store, with a canvas bag full of lentils, cucumber kefir, almond milk and soy chorizo, I lingered at the used book display table.

I'd been thinking a lot about experimental literature, and I'd been reading a book called *The Art of Recklessness* by Dean Young, a celebration of authorial wildness, risk-taking, and the imagination. And I noticed, there at Mt. Baker Books, a hardbound copy of James Joyce's *Finnegans Wake.* "Now there is risk-taking," I thought. There is the *something new* which Joyce had been brave enough to publish. Experimental? Of course. Successful? Well, who knows . . . critics and readers disagree. Worth giving it a try or two (or three)? Definitely.

I had a paperback copy at home which was past its prime. If I got a copy which presented itself elegantly to the world (even if it did lack the original cover) could I read it beginning-to-end as I'd never been able to before? What I actually needed was an annotated copy to guide me through. But meanwhile, I thought, this serious copy, with its business-suit navy blue binding, silver printing on the spine (saying all it needed to say: James Joyce. Finnegans Wake. Viking) would do. I was convinced by its heft and its apparent gravitas that the book deserved more effort than I had given it.

The price on the inside (lovely end-papers—bright and cheerful, grass-green) said $6.00, reduced from $12.00. A bargain! Still, I resisted. Should I buy another book with too many books at home already? With the house sinking into the ground under the weight of all those books?

But I opened it and turned to what I thought was going to be the title page. At the top, *upside down*, were the words "Paris / 1922-1939" and at the bottom of the page, upside down, was the page number: 540. Also upside down were the final non-sensical sentences (of an eight-page-long upside-down final paragraph):

We pass through grass behush the bush to. Finn, again!

Take. Bussftlhee, mememormee! Till thousandthee. Lps. The keys to. Given! A way a lone a last a loved a long the

Confused, I turned a few more pages—all were upside down. I considered the possibility that the copy in my hands had been printed in Great Britain, which often places the title sideways from bottom to top, rather than top to bottom as is done in the United States. Maybe I had just opened the book incorrectly? But no, that wasn't possible. The printing wouldn't be upside down in that case. I flipped the book over, turned it "upside down" (actually, right side up?) to what should have been the last page of the book. There was the title page: James Joyce, it said, not upside down. And in slightly smaller letters, Finnegans Wake. At the bottom: The Viking Press. New York. The book had been bound upside-down, presenting itself backwards.

Gravitas went flying out the door of that grocery store. I actually laughed out loud. Here was Joyce's *Finnegans Wake*, a grand classic of the Read-These-Books-Before-You-Die list, which few people have ever been able to read, a notoriously difficult book, bound upside-down. What a monumental screw-up on the part of who-knows-who, what an expensive mistake, and what a total delight. Perfect book for this perfect nose-smashing stumble. The Viking Press print run in 1959 had bound this print run (I hope it was thousands of copies) upside down. Did someone lose his job? Now, that's not too funny. There can be serious consequences for inattention. Or maybe the mistake was acceptable, less rare than I thought? An occasional print run must go wonky. Still, this was *Finnegans Wake*. The unintelligible classic. And the idea of it being in my hands, upside-down, backwards and, as a result, even less intelligible, was lovely.

Needless to say, I bought the book. What could be more irresistible than an unreadable copy of an unreadable book? And the more I thought about it, the more it seemed like a non-mistake, to have this risky book bound in a risky binding, as if to say "If you want this book because the story is new, fresh, challenging, risk-taking, experimental, we applaud you, and we offer you this new, fresh, challenging, risk-taking, experimental upside-down binding in return."

I've found a special place on my bookshelf for this book, which came along at the perfect moment for me. I'd recently finished writing a review of Eleni Sikelianos's lovely new book, *Make Yourself Happy*, for the online journal *Numéro Cinq*. My heart and mind were occupied with trying to understand exactly why Sikelianos was being called an "experimental" poet. She herself, in response to an interview question for the journal, had said, "I was on the radio last month, and the radio host introduced me as an 'experimental poet' about fifty times. My graduate students who heard it wondered why he couldn't just say 'poet.' I'm not that interested in categories in this regard. [. . .]"

I was also in the middle, as I've said, of reading (and loving) Dean Young's *The Art of Recklessness*, in which he celebrates the imagination and the articulation of "the foreign, the strange, the other." At one point, Young looks at children in the primary grades, their un-cowed experimentation with language, and he provides us not only with a great explanation of tired poetry ("When art strives for the decorums of craft, it withers to table manners during a famine") but a strong attempt to explain what poetry really is:

> Poetry is not a discipline. It's a hunger, a revolt, a drive, a mash note, a fright, a tantrum, a grief, a hoax, a debacle, an application, an affect. It is a collaboration: the bad news may be that we are never in control but the good news is that we collaborate with a genius—the language!

By the time I bought the badly bound *Finnegans Wake*, the dictionary definition of "experiment" was taped above my computer:

> **experiment (n.)**: mid-14c., "action of observing or testing; an observation, test, or trial;" also "piece of evidence or empirical proof; feat of magic or sorcery," from Old French esperment "practical knowledge, cunning; enchantment, magic spell; trial, proof, example; lesson, sign, indication," from Latin experimentum "a trial, test, proof, experiment," noun of action from experiri "to try, test," from ex- "out of"

(see <u>ex-</u>) + peritus "experienced, tested," from PIE *per-yo-, suffixed form of root <u>*per- (3)</u> "to try, risk."

There was that bottom line, the final word: *risk.* Not safe. <u>NOT SAFE.</u> Had I been playing things too safe for too long? The more I thought about language and safety, the more I understood what Sikelianos went on to say in the *Numéro Cinq* interview:

> "Experimental" is kind of a stand-in word for a number of things, one of which might be writing that creates meanings as it makes itself, rather than heading toward predetermined meaning. [. . .] So, a kind of writing that allows the tentative nature of the world into its proceedings, that admits that meaning and reality aren't fixed and sets out to test them, to discover and to try (the root meaning of "experiment").

It seemed to me that finding an upside-down copy of a convoluted book testified to that "tentative nature of the world." Reality, fixed or unfixed? The mistake of the binding: careless mistake or titillating addendum to Joyce's words, "Bussftlhee, mememormee!"? What pleased me was how appropriate the mistake was, despite its unintentionality.

Authorial intention, of course, usually enters into the discussion. Most writers, even brave writers, I think, believe in intentionality. Their work is theirs, their meanings are hopefully understood. But experimentation with language has gone barreling past intentionality, right into the fast lane of technology, hypertext and code work, some of it randomly generated. Can the random be intentional?

So—"experimental" writing. Those pesky quotation marks—why do I rely on them? Maybe because I believe that all poets worth their salt are experimenters? Recently, I've been questioning line breaks, since line breaks give writers permission to call something a poem even if the writing itself employs few poetic tools. Lazy, unexciting poetry (that is, poetry which takes no risks and finds no new ways to say things, no new convergences, no traditions made more exciting by the interruption of tradition, no moments of upside-down bindings) uses the line break as a safety net. Children being taught about poetry in elementary school learn that if they see line breaks, they're looking at a poem. Really—can that be true? Cliché-driven language, broken into lines—that's poetry? I don't think so. And if not, then what happens if you erase the line break? Do the clichés show up more? Maybe. But here's what I think can happen if things go well—you can retain all the play with sound, but present the poem as a line of prose, as I try to do in this very short poem:

Land

Beneath my feet, liquefaction, sinkholes, the sea rises, the sea subsides. I'm either high and dry or low and wet. And yet.

This could easily be a cinquain. Five lines, four line breaks. But I looked for something from the poetic toolbox besides line breaks to identify it as a poem: musicality, rhythms, metaphor. It seems a tiny bit risky for me to leave out the line breaks I might once have included. Needless to say, I lack both Joyce's brain and his bravura (I hear a voice saying, "Baby steps, Julie"). Does the elimination of line breaks challenge me (and readers) to search beyond easy designations for what is poetic? It does. Does a fresh layout fit the definition of "experimental"? L*A*N*G*U*A*G*E poetry it is not, but a poem—is it a poem? Just to be able to ask the question feels good, feels playful. Feels experimental.

So thank you, Viking Press 1959. *Finnegans Wake*, upside-down and backwards. My bet is Joyce would have laughed, too.

17
99 Preparatory Notes to Experimental Literature
Daniel Levin Becker

1. Attempted landings.

2. Is *experimental literature* an oxymoron or a redundancy?

3. That which chases its tail into the future.

4. The success of an experiment as the degree to which something new is learned about the world.

5. To prove it can be done.

6. Gratification disorder.

7. The absence of reliable psychographic indicators of what kind of person will say *the data is* and what kind *the data are*.

8. What happens when I push this button?

9. Literature as that which resists the empirical.

10. *If it can be done, why do it?*

11. Can 99 preparatory notes sufficiently prepare anyone for anything?

12. Maybe just one of those terms that no longer means what it means.

13. Inquisitive literature, curious literature, petulant literature, literature of the yes but.

14. Or that it can't.

15. Whose job is it to put interestingness into a text?

16. Experimental literature as that which, in some critical way, has not finished becoming.

17. *To the extent that the book has a structure, it resembles a Rubik's Cube that has not been solved.*

18. The journey of self-discovery is a litany of insults.

19. Attentive lardings.

20. Is *experimental* an epithet or a punch line?

21. The way all practitioners except the most dogged refuse to self-identify as such.

22. Like hipsters or emo bands.

23. Like *republican* or *disinterest.*

24. An experiment whose magic is in the finding, not the findings.

25. *This sublime and difficult novel—difficult now for the reader, but first for me—*

26. Or simply literature that flies by the seat of its pants.

27. The tipping point in the genesis of each project where the author determines that conventional form will not suffice to achieve the desired results.

28. Malcolm Gladwell's *The Tipping Point* as a work of experimental literature.

29. Would you like to come up and see my experimental Japanese etchings?

30. *I know it when I see it.*

31. Experimental literature as an attempt to find new knobs in language that can be tuned in order to alter reality in a real way.

32. Whatever *real* means.

33. *As poetry, it doesn't have to be good. It only has to contain a testable guess about being alive.*

34. The colon missing from *Life A User's Manual.*

35. Since 2001 I have kept a list of two-word phrases I like.

36. Beveled suture.

37. If there are desired results to begin with.

38. Does every excellent work of experimental literature make its hypothesis manifest at the outset?

39. What kind of pants does literature wear?

40. Jacques Roubaud claims he would not have joined the Oulipo had it retained its original name, *Séminaire de Littérature Expérimentale*.

41. Literature as the flunkey who spills coffee all over the lab table, compromising the scientific integrity of the experiment.

42. [*Gasp*] My experimental quiche!

43. The scene in *Dead Poets Society* where Robin Williams makes his students rip out the page of their textbooks detailing a mathematical method for evaluating the excellence of a poem.

44. *Fâcheuse lacune.*

45. Experimental proofs of the need for linearity and also of the need for anarchy.

46. 'Pataphysics and the poignant lack of coincidence that those people most committed to absurdity and inscrutability also had the biggest hard-on for bureaucracy.

47. *As if there were a control / so marvelous // you could teach it / to eat pain*

48. Untoward appropriations.

49. What if the question is *what is literature* and the hypothesis *everything*? I have long found this to be an extremely compelling interpretation of the term, and a beautiful, albeit monumentally distracting, way of looking at the world.

50. And this button?

51. Schrödinger's car.

52. What does the form of 99 preparatory notes, created and

practiced to measurably superlative effect by Frédéric Forte, ask about the world?

53. Is a list of two-word phrases data?

54. Experimental literature as, contrary to orthodox usage, that which is utterly conventional in every formal sense but is genuinely capable of effecting experimentation among its readers.

55. Reading a self-help book as experimental literature.

56. Allow me to answer you through experimental interpretive dance.

57. *If the poem's score for perfection is plotted on the horizontal of a graph and its importance is plotted on the vertical, then calculating the total area of the poem yields the measure of its greatness.*

58. Not long ago my father remarked that I seemed so worried about my epitaph I was neglecting to live my life.

59. *The way fashion is never finished.*

60. If you had found this list scrawled on a piece of paper discarded on a busy street.

61. Writing a self-help book as experimental literature.

62. *at an early age I'd somehow chosen to cast my lot with my life's drama's supposed audience instead of with the drama itself*

63. Experimental literature as the sum total of attempts to clone the entire wraparound sensibility of the author, and bestow it completely upon the reader, in the space of a single text.

64. A kite on a peaceful day.

65. The glum suspicion that, literature being literature, the success or failure of any such experiment can be evaluated only with metrics that are wholly intuitive and affective and unempirical.

66. The problem of subjective science.

67. The problem of private art.

68. The problem of private parts.

69. Part primate.

70. Pasta primavera.

71. Penne alla vodka.

72. Versace Versace.

73. Excuse me.

74. This button?

75. 'Pataphysics as "the science of imaginary solutions."

76. Literature as that which has standardized its refusal of standardization.

77. Experimental proofs of the possibility of exhaustion and also of the impossibility of closure.

78. *Life Everlasting—based on a misprint!*

79. Whalehearted approbation.

80. The Turing test as extended metaphor for experimental literature, or vice versa.

81. If the overarching experimental quarry of science is to defeat immortality, what is the overarching experimental quarry of literature?

82. Ah yes, same thing.

83. *I do not like clock(s).*

84. Punitive wanglings.

85. *Probably you are walking with your husband in SoHo, seeing what the new artists are refusing to do there, in their quest for a scratch to start from.*

86. Rip it out!

87. What do(es) my data mean to you?

88. My desire to correct *epitaph* to *obituary*.

89. My desire to correct *problem* to *beauty*.

90. *Commendably futile.*

91. Experimental proofs of the need to overthrow the tyranny of artifice and also of a deep-rooted fondness for and essence-permeating dependence upon artifice.

92. *The brotherhood of man on earth will be possible only on a basis of kitsch.*

93. Can reality be broadcast and remain real?

94. A litany of insults.

95. *That would be terribly disappointing—if God were to prove to be an electron.*

96. Experimental literature as the sum total of attempts to materialize the *it* one knows when one sees, in the measurably more or measurably less desperate hope that one can get someone else to see it too.

97. To prove it can be done.

98. yes I said yes it can Yes.

99. What about this bu

18
"Go and keep halting progress!"
Mark Lipovetsky

I'll be writing about the Russian brand of experimental literature, since this is what I know best and since I believe that this experience, thanks to its idiosyncratic character, might reveal some otherwise hidden aspects of experimental literature as a universal cultural phenomenon.

Allegedly, or rather according to legend, Osip Mandelstam used to say that Russia (or in his case, the Soviet Union) was the last place where literature had preserved its true value—because writers could still be killed for their work. His own tragic life and even more tragic death proved him right. Mandelstam meant that literature in Russia possesses so much symbolic capital that political powers either try to use it for their own means (what was called Socialist Realism) or, if that doesn't work, eliminate the unruly competitors. From the standpoint of Stalinist cultural officialdom and the few generations to follow (while Mandelstam's poems circulated in samizdat), he was "a poet for poets," i.e., his poetry supposedly represented a clear-cut case of experimental literature.

But was it actually experimental? Looking at Mandelstam's (or Anna Akhmatova's, or Joseph Brodsky's) poetics with an unbiased eye, one may be surprised to notice its intentional archaism. Certainly, archaism can be experimental as well—the story of the Russian avant-garde, from Natalia Goncharova and Mikhail Larionov's neo-primitivist paintings to Velimir Khlebnikov's futuristic invention of a Pra-Slavonic vocabulary—are quite telling in this respect. But Mandelstam was not just archaic, he was neo-*classical*, i.e., he sought to establish a dialogue between the catastrophic contemporary and well-established examples of classical harmony in art, literature and architecture, and that is exactly why he irritated the authorities so much.

The story of Daniil Kharms unfolds simultaneously with Mandelstam's, for Kharms perished in a Leningrad prison hospital a few years after Mandelstam's death in one of the gigantic Gulag camps. Kharms, the original creator of Russian absurdism in poetry, prose and drama, an eccentric and dark trickster, and a master at disrupting logic, syntax, and the limits of the imagination, has been read and studied no less than Mandelstam. Kazimir Malevich blessed Kharms with the inscription on his book (enigmatic at best): "Go and keep halting progress!" Some read this as a call to resist modernity with its fetishization of rationality and the idea of progress, others evoke it as proof of Malevich's disappointment in the Soviet quasi-scientific utopia. In either case, Kharms was doing exactly what Malevich wanted him to do: challenging modernity's logos, questioning rationality's solid truth, mocking authoritative discourses—and therefore, creating experimental literature.

One may argue that Kharms and Mandelstam alike were persecuted because of their radical difference from the social and cultural norms enforced in the Soviet habitus. Indeed, they both were natural nonconformists who physically could not write "normal" texts, even when they tried. However, from what we know about Kharms today, the Stalinist authorities, unlike us, did not take his writings very seriously—maybe because they were so hilarious? Those who came to arrest him in 1941 did not even confiscate his whole archive, although that was an otherwise customary procedure. His biographer calls this a miracle: thanks to the NKVD's negligence, Kharms' manuscripts and notebooks survived and reached the next generation(s). In contrast with this incident, one may recall Nadezhda Mandelstam's heroic effort to save her arrested husband's archive—partially memorized by her, and partially hidden by loyal friends.

Probably, from the point of view of the authorities, Kharms—with his experimental writings—was not a poet per se.

They preferred to treat his writings as a reflection of his mental instability, rather than as anything of literary value. In effect, the symbolic power of Kharms's works was, from the standpoint of the political authorities, too insignificant to worry about, presenting no competing discourses.

This certainly did not save Kharms, but doesn't it testify to a specific status intrinsic to Russian experimental literature? The latter does not appear capable or desirous of commanding symbolic power—or any other for that matter. It rejects power from the start. It might pursue many diverse experimental vectors or projects, but power is never one of them. Following this definition of experimental literature à la Russe, a true experimental writer would be, for example, Vladimir Nabokov, but not Vladimir Mayakovsky. Nabokov with his disgust for the "Literature of Ideas"—or literature seeking to exercise symbolic power over the masses—believed that instead of grand ideas, literature should focus on "aesthetic bliss, that is a sense of being somehow, somewhere, connected with other states of being where art (curiosity, tenderness, kindness, ecstasy) is the norm." Mayakovsky, despite his early period's exuberant experimentation, stops being experimental when he, along with the other "left Futurists," lends his voice and his idiom to be utilized by Soviet political power. He kills himself when he realizes the failure of that attempt and that his offer is ignored by the authorities; but in fact, he erred. His avant-gardist idiom was indeed adopted by the Soviet discourse of power, albeit castrated and inscribed into the Socialist Realist canon. There could be other scenarios, of course. Sergei Tretiakov, Mayakovsky's colleague in the avant-garde journal *LEF* and Bertolt Brecht's friend, also wanted to "speak Bolshevik," or rather to teach others how to master that skill. He perished during the Great Terror because he was too close to politics; the authorities vigilantly safeguarded their turf from unauthorized intrusions.

Do I place too much trust in the critical judgment of the authorities, or even worse, the so-called "competent organs," whose competence was largely limited to expertise in torture and sadism? To avoid that impression, let us consider another example coming from a much more "vegetarian" (albeit not entirely safe) era of the 1970s-80s. The attitude to radically experimental literature remained the same as in the 1920s-50s: it was not published, despite the fact that Andrei Voznesensky, with his soft-edged experimentalism, published freely and served as the international face of liberal Soviet literature. Even more curiously, a son of the KGB general responsible for control over the "creative intelligentsia" was a big fan of Velimir Khlebnikov, and therefore books of his poetry imitating the historical avant-garde were published in the most popular Soviet presses.

At that time, Dmitri Prigov, a leading figure of the Moscow underground art and literary scene, a man of many trades as a poet, visual and performance artist, novelist, and theorist, was not published in the USSR until the Perestroika period. However, he and his circle of friends were distinct from many other artists and writers in the underground in totally lacking interest in publishing and receiving official acknowledgement. That was an intentional rejection of any ambition to power, symbolic or otherwise, which served as the core condition of Prigov's literary and performative experiments. Prigov's entire oeuvre—consisting, by the way, of thousands of texts in various genres—is a monumental *Gesamtkunstwerk* mocking the entire body of literature based on striving for symbolic power. Certainly, this is a global parody of Russian literature with its writer-prophets and spiritual leaders. But not only, not only. . . .

I do not want to absolutize this feature. Russian culture is famous for its quasi-religious attitude to literature and its creators—the so-called "literature-centrism" (as opposed to Derridian logocentrism). I am arguing, however, that within this cultural milieu, literary experimentation is more valuable when it subverts, inverts, or blatantly assaults the most historically solid and deeply normalized aspects of national culture. In Russian culture, a demonstrative abdication of the writer's place of power and authority radicalizes experiments with a new language and vision. On the contrary, in American poetry, where the poet has long ago given up the will to (political) power, the forceful intervention of poetry into the field of politics, borne by a charismatic voice and authoritative position, would be a congruently radical form of experimentation.

In short, literary experimentation is truly successful only when it confronts supposed cultural "constants," the most solid parts of the given nation's cultural imaginary. Otherwise, it is doomed to remain a purely technical affair.

19
The Zoo We Thought We Bought Bought Us: How the Shape
of Shape Shapes Us
Michael Martone

It Looks Like That

In 1978, the Seattle architectural firm of Jones and Jones
published their revolutionary work, "Gorilla Habitat,
Comprehensive Plan, Woodland Park Zoo." The plan, based on
"landscape immersion," sought to construct a zoo that was not a
zoo, disguising the apparatus of captivity and confusing artfully
the distinction between the animal on view and the one doing the
viewing. Ten years later in an *Atlantic* article, Melissa Greene
refers to a letter sent by Dian Fossey, the famed primatologist and
consultant on the project, who had shown photographs of the
Seattle exhibit to her colleagues at the scientific station in
Rwanda, reporting that they were convinced the photos of
gorillas at the zoo were taken in the wild. Fossey, as a
consultant, had flown to Washington state. Driving in from the
airport, David Hancocks, the principle of the project, recalls they
were anxious to get from her a sense of what the Rwandan
highland rainforest looked like. Fossey, pointing out the car's
windows, said, "It looks like that! It looks just like that!" The
designers learned from that encounter that they could stop
"designing" and let the native plants go native, be invasive,
naturalizing the exhibit. And they did.

Mopping Up

Brothers and Sisters, my text today is not drawn from the books of Bakhtin or Shklovsky. Instead, let's open our missals to the verses of St. Thomas Kuhn and *The Structures of Scientific Revolutions*. Kuhn argued that science progressed through a series of paradigm shifts not in a continuous linear fashion. Once the paradigm of physics, say, is in place he argued, science busies itself mainly with "mopping up" the details of the phenomenon the paradigm defines. Individual experiments never overthrow the paradigm but reaffirm the paradigm's initial elegance and predictive nature. That is to say, most of science isn't so much about discovering new knowledge as it is about corroborating and collaborating with the paradigm. Scientists hate Kuhn as Kuhn depicts most of what they do as not original but custodial. Scientists get testy when pictured merely testing the veracity of the paradigm not testing the phenomenon itself.

Many of us write our books in or near, cheek to jowl with, university and college labs. To what extent do we labor in the structuring of our books—let's call them novels—in a paradigmatic way, or do we work in the form as a received and clearly defined paradigm? Are we when we write a novel, even a novel that experiments with such elements as relativistic point-of-view, time, tense, transparency or self-consciousness, "mopping-up"? The formal innovations we seek to introduce might be seen from the remove of the paradigm as mere tweaks to the structure. This behemoth superstructure absorbs the tinkering as part of the already fabricated form that is defined as "Novel." This Novel overstories our mere understorying stories. Like our scientific colleagues, we labor in the belief our efforts are original when they are, in fact, fully expected and anticipated. The cultural expectations are for the writer to be mainly curatorial, to contribute to the Novel paradigm, the tradition of the novel. The real action of innovative shape-changing is not within the genre but at the level of genre. We think we are the keepers of the zoo that houses the novel when in fact we might be kept by the zoo that is the novel.

I Can Say I Wrote This Paper

For example. I can say I wrote this paper, that I am the originator
of this paper, and in writing a paper about other shapes the writer
of a novel might deploy beyond the narrative, I, the writer of this
paper, thought I would incorporate structural disruptions and
participatory flourishes into the text's flow to demonstrate
alternative means of structuring "a paper," extrapolating such
formal innovations into the target novel form.
I can say I wrote this paper, but to what extent can we all
say that the conference steering committee of AWP "wrote" this
paper. Or more exactly to what extent can we say that they
structured the form of the paper, a matrix, if you will, a lath onto
which I trowel a text. To what extent was this paper written
already for me by the AWP?
I wrote this paper, but to what extent can I say that the
management and employees of the Hilton Hotel Company who
have constructed the fixed form of the delivery device of said
paper wrote it? To what extent was the form of my paper and its
delivery dictated, not by me, but by the building codes of the
municipality of the City of Chicago enforced by the attentive eye
of its fire marshal?

The Thor Tool Decision

In *Thor Power Tool Company v. Commissioner*, 439 U.S 522 (1979) the United States Supreme Court upheld IRS regulations limiting how taxpayers could write down inventory and in so doing rewrote the form of the American novel. Prior to the Thor decision a publisher's backlist was its most valuable asset. Once that inventory could not be written down, a publisher's frontlist was its only asset and forced the need to produce instantly profitable blockbusters that justified the expense of warehousing. Publishers could no long afford to sell a few hundred copies of a "good" book a year, year after year. Such books were pulped or sold into the remainder market. A consequence of this 1979 decision, the year I graduated a master in literary fiction, was the rise of Barnes & Noble whose business specialized in selling remaindered books. In Thor, the court existentially changed the nature of publishing's business model and in an interesting coincidence corresponded to a cultural and artistically critical discussion of the death of the novel. The novel survived of course by seeking refuge in nonprofit publishing enterprises or by becoming commercially viable in the new business environment. The individual writers of novels may believe that the series of aesthetic choices they make are theirs to make but those choices are influenced subtly and not so subtly by these larger nonartistic structures and strictures, conglomerations of economic and political forces that force the writer to adapt or cloister. That cloistering comes, of course, with its own stints, constraints, and demands—think tenure and patronage policies. We may arrange the spaces inside these cages, our offices, our departments. Look, the dappled light spilling through the barred and shuttered windows casts a dappled shadow on the pages on which we write. Film Noir was not the original invention of the auteur of the genre but a structured response to the imposition of the Hayes Office's censorship codes.

The Structure for This Paper Was Predetermined

The structure for this paper was predetermined. One of its strictures was that it be 15 minutes in length. Fifteen minutes in length to accommodate four papers, introductions of their authors, and time for questions. I choose to burn now one of my fifteen minutes with one minute of silence. Timekeeper.

The Sex Life of the Musk Ox

Hey! What a good-looking audience! Anybody from the University of Alaska, Fairbanks? I spent a week there once as a visiting writer and wrote in what was a profoundly different cultural and material substrate generating fictive narrative. Forget for a minute monstrous vegetables grown in the college gardens. Forget for a minute the young Japanese couples who visit to copulate, it is believed fortuitously, beneath the Northern Lights. Forget for a minute that light to dark ratio does not vary day-to-day by minutes but by quarter hours. Forget for a minute that writers live in cabins with no running water, as buried pipes would melt the tundra. Forget for a minute that writers are propelled by means of dog-powered skijoring and that room is made in each classroom for said dogs to relax and rough-house together before the journey to the next class. All strange indeed. But consider what the journeyman writers of the University of Alaska, Fairbanks attend to for their RA stipend. That is really strange. Manning camouflaged huts on the four corners of a vast enclosure they observe the musky sex lives of the musk ox, a procedure described to me as the determined mounting of one haystack onto another. I imagine the love stories generated by the close and endless observation of such ground hugging clouds, the plodding plotting on the gridded maps of space, the rendezvous of a prehistoric species brought back from the brink of extinction to infect our own cowed dreams.

I Have Always Wanted You to Admire My Fasting

"'Well, clear this out now!' said the overseer, and they buried the hunger artist, straw and all. Into the cage they put a young panther. Even the most insensitive felt it refreshing to see this wild creature leaping around the cage that had so long been dreary. The panther was all right. The food he liked was brought to him without hesitation by the attendants; he seemed not even to miss his freedom..."

To the caged animal the cage is just the cage. It is by definition nonmalleable, immutable, irresistible, static. Artists in the cage, we bend, we change, we adapt to the discipline of the cage, do not miss our freedom as much as welcome the confining definition of the structures we inhabit. When the cage is just a cage it is perfectly disguised as a cage. It is the embodiment of off-limits limits. We have room to frolic, to bound in our bounded precincts. We look through the bars to see the other animals seemingly enmeshed in their own cages. We look and they look, but both of us, caught up in our cages of seeing, see no other way to see.

20
Alive
Carole Maso

The experimental has always been about finding the way to stay alive on the page, open to radiance and vibrancy and the infinite possibilities of word and world. A vertiginous free fall into beauty, it follows no god, worships no formula—one sets out in the night on an adventure (*the lake*), toward the unknown, embracing uncertainty, courting ruin, following an intuition, a premonition—stumbling after something—thrilling, ineffable, in motion, becoming, yet-to-be, never before seen. Mysterious and inviting, seductive, one might time and space travel or move not at all—stay small within the confines of a syllable or two. We might try to shape emotion like music or apply a glittering geometrics or calculus to the proceedings. The openness is all. Neither inherited or borrowed, it resists the death impulse that drives so much mainstream work, with its desire to be little and safe and over and already decided. One might allow in the unbidden or the tangential or the random. Invited: endless permutation and variability. At once playful and grave.

And we take our experiments into the lab. We may test a series of thresholds, or weaknesses—note the things we might otherwise swerve away from or circle. We might place our vulnerability into a crucible. Watch the way a narrative given the chance might fray. We might place darkness inside and chronicle 7 Tenebrae responses. We might subject our text to fire or ice or ultraviolet light. Explore the effects of freezing—what does it do to the temporal: the synchronic, the simultaneous? Or fire— reconstitute what we can from the char. Working with the embers:

the residue, the trace. That which is left in the end. Bring our heartbreak. Be not afraid: Into the strangeness and the sorrow *(she died without warning, out of time, in her sleep during the winter break)* the limitation of the mortal body *(and in my heart a glass globe—that is how I picture it)*. Placed in a cradle that holds time, our experiments might be with brevity or density or with the way things end.

Last semester, we read in my freshman seminar Georges Perec's *An Attempt at Exhausting a Place in Paris* (*1982*). And only weeks later, after the Paris bombings, we read it again, and talked about the flexibility of a text and the way meaning accumulates and the melancholy of ordinary things and the weight of the world and 13 ways to not look away. To create a vessel to hold all this, to contain all that is uncontainable. The things we think impossible to bear or understand. Traversing the uncertain, the open-ended, the strange forever in us.

We might find the way. We might write in codes—in talking codes or computer codes or in the love notes we once passed in class so long ago. We might attempt an accordion narrative, a bifurcated novel, or a story like an echo chamber. We might find ourselves up against the inexorable until something gives way and the narrative blooms or transforms or levitates.

We'll invite the unexpected in, the outlandish, the unbidden. Tolerant of the erasure, the tangential, the mysterious, the right road lost. We'll leave nothing out—or maybe we'll leave almost everything out.

In the laboratory today—an assignment for my undergrads—take your name and see what it has to reveal. The secret asleep in that configuration—and write a piece. Discover these intimacies and connections and reverberations. The thing you have carried all this time, the first word you ever heard—your name. Or on another day, begin with a sharply focused, clearly delineated story and keep adjusting the lens and chronicle that slowly moving out of focus until you end with a blur. There are endless things to test and try—because we are alive.

And after a day's work, and upon reflection, when asked to reflect, it seems to me the experimental involves a different sort of engagement with the page than the mainstream's engagement. It interrogates assumptions, as it always has. In active dialog with the things the mainstream has guarded so fiercely and taken for granted—story, content, syntax form. The experimental is engaged with the passionate scrutiny of the sentence, the paragraph, and the chapter. It asks, among many other things, what the novel might be. An inquiry as fresh and urgent as it's ever been.

The experimental departs with the mainstream also in its interactions and its grappling with silence. Silence—that thing at the heart of all expression—the thing that is always there presiding, against which we shimmer and come into being—for our allotted time. Silence, something formulaic writing blithely ignores. The mainstream has fallen asleep and there is no awakening it. It is flattened by it, swallowed and consumed by it, and left forgotten. For it is the silence that informs the shapes we make. We write into it bravely and with daring and folly, charmed by the unsayable, and all we are up against. The silence—

which is deafening.

and surely here to devour us.

into the abyss we go.

we may not make it back.

And still we were alive to it and made lively exchanges with it and bargains and sometimes we employed desperate measures, and other times we decorated it or just danced, and the attempt was everything here in our one and only moment on earth.

Our moment: I ask my freshmen to print out their twitter accounts to use as narratives. We think about compression and patterns and offhandedness. And what we make without realizing it.

Our moment: From afar the drones create a new feeling in this new century. How might we find a language for it. That strangeness. How to engage with moral injury—the way we hurt now—and the hope fueled desire through language and shape to heal—still.

Our moment: The destruction of cultural artifacts, it wears on us—civilization's erasure.

Our moment: The person you knew who vanishes at the mysterious mid point traversing the spectrum of gender. Right there before you and also not at all.

Our moment: News of more terrorist attacks arrive pixelated on a small screen held in the palm of a human hand. The galaxy is drifting apart. We write against the flood. The great melting. Or a world in flames. And our perishing. In the crucible: our perishing.

(*She died without warning before the spring semester. She left without telling us.*)

And all those vaporized that September day in New York. Emerging from the fog now—A blue bowl or a lake. Listen: I hear sighing. There is the lover again at the wordless place. She ambles through a labyrinth, a maze—hedges, a row of trees or double skyscrapers. I might choose to follow her. An experimental text might allow her to live at the cusp of legibility. Glimpsed. Her pale blue scarf in the wind and her hair...

In class we watch *My Winnipeg* (*2007*). In class we read Anna Kavan. We listen to Kanye West. In class we create Cornell boxes in prose. Or after Bachelard, we make our own poetics of space. We are open to everything: the experiment might involve a collision of forms or the use of collage (*when we were children in the kitchen with our grandmother*), or changes of registers, or...We might try anything; we might do anything for there is nowhere on this earth where we are quite this free. With exuberance and passion and curiosity and joy and surprise, we forge on.

I bring in the (*disavowed*) research of Dr. Masararu Emoto (*born in Japan, 1947*) who performed a series of experiments observing the physical effect of words, prayers, music and environment on the crystalline structure of water with the understanding that water has a memory. Emoto hired photographers to take pictures of water after being exposed to the different variables and subsequently froze them so that they would form crystalline structures. Water before Mozart and water after Mozart. Water without words, water in which the word thank you is repeated continuously and with love.

We're bedazzled, lost, ecstatic, curious, incandescent, in transit. In communion with all that is within us and beside us, and outside us, in and out of reach. In love with risk and darkness and failure and beauty. For the brief and precious time we are here.

These days of wonder.

The experimental is alive and well. I think of my incredibly intrepid graduate students. They've been chosen for their abundant talent, and for what we suspect might be their willingness to stray far, to fail better, to trust their strangest intuitions and wildest hunches—to honor that which passes through them: every intimation, every figment, every future.

***

Yeji Ham
Brown MFA '16 Fiction

The number 304 on the door moved. A skirt swished. A loud grunt echoing in the hallway. Something about fat. Something about no more. A woman emerged from the apartment 304. The woman who lived with her husband and mother-in-law. Something about noise complaint. Something about sugar. The woman did not see G standing in the hallway. The woman pushed herself out of the door. Holding a purse on one hand. Holding her mother-in-law with another. Her mother-in-law, a kidney.

"can't do this,"

A kidney in the woman's grip.

"Why do you even want to go outside?"

The woman locked the door.

The kidney trembled as if coughing.

G stayed close to the wall. Leaning right up against the wall. Watching the dark red lump pulse in the woman's hands. The lump shaped like a bean. Bulging out of her fingers. Moist and slippery. The woman's fingers squeezed the kidney tighter. Telling her to stay still. Telling her mother-in-law to wait, wait for just a few seconds more. The woman looked up. Smiling at G. G stood still. The woman laughed.

"My mother-in-law," she shook her head, "she's become more difficult."

The woman had lived with her mother-in-law for more than eleven years.

"Always complaining," the woman said, "always complaining that I don't put enough salt in the dish. Or something's too raw. Or a maid stole her necklace. She comes to my bed at night. Whispering to me, fire her, fire her, fire her."

Two years ago, paramedics pounded on G's apartment.

"We never had a maid," she said, "Maybe she thinks I am the maid."

At three in the morning.

"She would sometimes call me by Misses."

Travis Vick:
Brown MFA '16 Fiction
After sex (with love): The view of a path which stretches, like his or her body, out ahead of him—a path with rows of nameless trees on each side; tall trees, which lean to one another, creating a roof of some sort, or a small night. He loiters at the beginning of the path, with his hands in his pockets. There he looks down the path as far as he can, lonely, like someone lost in a hotel hallway. He assumes he knows where the path leads. He can imagine what will be at the end—so that, when words return, a small list of what would *not* have been there may be made: wicker chairs in a garden, a pulling of wind, some laundry-line of outgrown dresses. Nothing to see for himself.

Katy Mongeau:
Brown MFA '16 Fiction
A call like a bird that is not a bird. The son and the father are underway. My footprints gone muddy with the swamp's forgiving floor, but how long until they find me? Their boots romping the forest's shallow growths. A nearby mockingbird calls out to tell them. The blood of a bird when I am a bird. The bird as a god-fearing fly. I am the bird, I am the fly and I have no faith in distinctions.

...When first tried to speak after seeing her there, I let out a sigh so drawn and light. I thought I lost my life. Still I clenched my mask between my teeth. I used the language I'd always known. I kept me in English, my own separate badness.

Inside the ocean is every glyph, and the friction of their

moving makes a rupture of sound that we call the background of the world. A curse is made in ochre signs that make themselves. They're careful we can't make them. In the space between wonder and blasphemy is me.

21
Experimental
Steve McCaffery

In my own estimation, the term "experimental" is more
appropriate to scientific than literary endeavors; its implications
include a tentative stance, a testing, uncertainty, trial and error. I
concur most heartily with the late British novelist B. S. Johnson's
response to a question posed him as to whether or not his own work
was experimental. The gist of his reply was that all his experiments
end up in the waste paper basket. A catena of alternative synonyms
suggest themselves: investigative, deviant, exploratory, unor-
thodox, egregious, anomalous, avant-garde, any of the above. My
preferred term is investigative and my own sense of
"experimental" would be invention arrived at via investigation. It
is tempting to equate experimental with that great desideratum of
Modernism: innovation. But how is something new? My critical
book, *Darkness of the Present* (2012), attempts to perform an
archaeology upon the "now" and to open up the anachronic within
claims to innovation sufficient to modify the "new" not as *de facto*
but along the lines of Michel Foucault's notion of "truth effects."
There are literary formations that have the effect of being new
without necessarily being so. One example comes to mind.
William Burroughs's cut-up technique which he acknowledged
derived from Bryon Gysin's cut-up paintings. However, it has a
blatant predecessor: an eighteenth-century poetry miscellany *The
Foundling Hospital of Wit* (1743-49) prints an early version of cut-
up by Caleb Whitefoord, whose "cross-readings" across the
columns of newspapers carry the same disjunctive effect.
I believe a historical continuity of "anomalous" literature

can be argued. Jumping in at a point other than an origin and in a strictly Anglophonic context I would claim James Shirley's seventeenth-century dice poems, Christopher Smart's *Jubilate Agno* (1759), William Blake's illuminated books, Erasmus Darwin's *The Botanic Garden* (1791), William Wordsworth and Samuel Taylor Coleridges's *Lyrical Ballads* (1798), some poetry of George Meredith and A. C. Swinburne, Gertrude Stein, Ezra Pound's *Cantos* (1925), Louis Zukofsky, Basil Bunting, as being genuinely inventive.

It's tempting too to allocate experimental to an evolutionary scheme: from mimesis (Plato), through didactic (Horace to Matthew Arnold) to Expression (Romanticism) to experimental (late nineteenth century). However, such apportioning is thwarted by difficulties and is over-simplistic to say the least. In any test case it seems one can either stress its continuity or emphasize its discontinuity. Aeschylus, for example, was the first dramatist to diminish the power of the chorus in Greek drama, just as Shakespeare was the first English playwright to both shatter the Aristotelian unities of time and place, and to intermingle comic events with tragic. Does that make them experimental writers?

It will be easiest for me to outline a few of my own "experiments" (investigations). Since at least 1966 I have been committed to poetry as an exploratory probe into both territories and epistemology, and from its beginnings back then my notions of poetics have been fertilized by readings within contemporary philosophy. Through my readings in Georges Bataille's work, especially his theory of the general economy and sacrifice, I began to rethink poetic form as poetic economy, the poem as a distribution of flows and intensities that would register through the foregrounding of elements of linguistic materiality. Gilles Deleuze's notion of "becoming," alongside François Lyotard's concept of "phrase linkage" as developed in his book *The Différend* (1983), led me into a search for a more dynamic alternative to the normative sentence: phrase propulsion. Let me quote a short passage from my long poem LAG to give you a sense of its dynamic yet segmentative nature:

one is left with a sound against the silence of the world,
Keats in a discotheque smears content as paraphrase, a left
side to residue, showing not saying, each laryngitic
        whispers
that tokens are truths, but hearing smell is too narrow,
shrewd not cheroot, the homo or the hetero diegetic tour
        guide
with his cat food schedule, dirt when immortal, no parts are
        the same

Later I formulated the concept of the parapoetic, conceived as an undetermined concept, governed by its non-definability and its trangression of frames and partitions. To give this a name relevant to the present call I'd name it experimental sprawl, a seeping over into other disciplines for ideas to transpose into the poetic field. A single poetic will draw influence along the trajectory of the knight's move as Victor Shklovsky outlines it, i.e. not from another poetics but from one or more other disciplines: architecture, nuclear physics, or lattice algebra. My own move took me into architectural theories, especially axionometric diagrams as a poetic model.

To shift to an ontological frame, collaboration per se might well be judged as experimental, a meeting of variant creativities and criticalities in an unknown space of production. This was exactly the case in my own collaborative ventures as a member of the sound poetry ensemble Four Horsemen from 1969 to 1988. The group comprised myself, Paul Dutton, bpNichol and Rafael Barreto-Rivera. Our scores were designed to offer us points of cohesion, moments to which we could (and would) return in order to bring about a kind of consonance, after extended forays into individual and sub-set improvisations and non-guided trajectories. For the nearly two decades of the group's existence, "poem making" was approached as an experiment in the construction of spontaneous community and carried beyond performance into constructing intersubjectivity and mutual respect. I coined a French word for this kind of relationship: *écouture*, an art of listening as opposed to writing (*écriture*) that brought silence into the performances as a shaping element. Another collaborative venture that might be considered experimental was my collaborative writing and research with bpNichol. Collectively, as the Toronto Research Group (or TRG) we investigated alternatives to the normative academic paper doing research into narrative, translation, performance and the search for non-narrative prose by way of written reports, but also performance. The most fascinating aspect of the collaboration was the actual method of transcription of the research. As an analogue project through the seventies and eighties (Nichol died in 1988) we would take turns sitting at a typewriter transcribing the other person's words and thoughts. On occasions, however, independent thoughts would arise in the typist and they would get transcribed; there was thus an element of undecidability.

Regarded quantitively, experimental writing must always be a minor writing and must occupy a margin, for where else would be an appropriate location? I will end by positing an alliance between feminism, romanticism and experimental literature. Hélène Cixous in her famous essay of the mid-seventies "The Laugh of the Medusa" (1975) defines woman by precisely her non-definablity, the same definition Friedrich Schlegel gives to romanticism: it's romantic when it can't be defined. Lyotard remarked somewhere that to "fix meaning once and for all that is what terror wants." So let's leave "experimental" a way out of such discourses that define and allow it in its various ways to bring back the future.

22

Decomposition FrameWords: Experimental Writing, Fictional Awareness and the Information Wars

Christina Milletti

In Alain Robbe-Grillet's experimental novel *Jealousy* (1957), the narrator spends a protracted amount of time describing a scene in a room where his wife and her lover are meeting. Standard stuff, any reader might think, for a novel with "jealousy" seemingly in the title. But in Robbe-Grillet's *nouveau roman*, emotions of any kind—rage, distrust, desire—are stripped away in order to highlight an aesthetic of strict observation. The narrator's gaze surveys the room with great detachment: he makes no distinctions between depictions of his "real" wife, her lover and their actions, and memories of the room that he knows well. Even the painted birds in canvassed flight on one wall receive equally attentive description, so that the real, the remembered, and the represented are portrayed in precisely the same light. In result, these normally varied layers of fiction are flattened, decomposed, into a contiguous surface of linguistic description that not only constitutes the "reality" of the book, but also arguably joins with, in Robbe-Grillet's experimental poetic, the bordering realm of his readers situated in their own related discursive realities. In other words, in Robbe-Grillet's fiction, the real and the imagined are not portrayed in opposition. They're instead presented as variable modes of expression. A controversial poetic at the time. Perhaps still.

Even now, due to the novel's historical bondage to issues of representation, the work of fiction generally remains circumscribed by its role as entertainment: the novel is still most often perceived as nothing more than a service genre with populist leanings, a safety valve designed to help readers escape their daily ennui. Humbert Humbert reminds us as much in the first lines of *Lolita* (1955). "You can always count on a murderer for a fancy prose style," he reflects, before Nabokov goes on to seduce us with acts of highwire linguistic playfulness, distracting readers in awe of the narrator's lyrical musings from the novel's core theme of pedophilia. In the end, *Lolita* is as much about sexual abuse as it is about the power of words to shape meaning—which is to say, to act on readers' perceptions. Something more than a story is being experienced in such a fiction, isn't it? What precisely has the novel done? What kinds of acts on the reader have taken place?

It was once contentious to propose that fiction can act on readers. Yet at this precise socio-political moment—as propaganda, lies, and "alternate facts" become commonplace encounters with fiction in everyday life creating divisiveness and confusion—I'd argue it is now crucial to understand how fictional language intersects with and operates on ordinary language and experience. When spin room jockeying becomes the approved praxis of powerful institutions, fiction itself becomes a "matter" of *fact*.

Fiction has always been measured by its relation, or divergence, from reality: how *real*, how *credible* a story is. Reality, conversely, is never measured by its relationship to fiction. Yet it's not too much to say that in recent days expectations of reality have changed, and, in result, the role and behavior of fiction has changed along with it. We have to start asking ourselves: has the nature of fiction been altered with respect to the times? Or is fiction beginning to reveal operations in its own construction that have always been there to exploit?

Above all: what, if anything, can be done about it?

FRAMEWORDS

Secretary of State Colin Powell, 2003
"Our conservative estimate is that Iraq today has a stockpile of between 100 and 500 tons of chemical weapons agent. That is enough to fill 16,000 battlefield rockets."

President George W. Bush, 2003
"Intelligence gathered by this and other governments leaves no doubt that the Iraq regime continues to possess and conceal some of the most lethal weapons ever devised."

Donald Trump, 2016
"In addition to winning the Electoral College in a landslide, I won the popular vote if you deduct the millions of people who voted illegally."

A SHORT HISTORY OF POWER, NARRATIVE, AND FICTIONAL AWARENESS

In her essay, "The Killers" (1993), Kathy Acker directly addresses the impact of realist literature on readers' socio-political views—how fiction orients our perceptions of the world around us. As she writes:

> If I'm going to tell you what the real is by mirroring it, by telling you a story that expresses reality, I'm attempting to tell you how things are. By letting you see through my own eyes, I give you viewpoints, moral, and political. In other words, realism is simply a control method. Realism doesn't want to negotiate, open into, chaos or the body or death, because those who practice realism want to limit their readers' perceptions, want to limit perceptions to a centric—which in this society is always a phallocentric—reality.... *In other words, behind every literary or cultural issue lies the political, the realm of political power. And whenever we talk about narration, narrative structure,*

we're talking about political power (my italics).

Acker's experimental fictions are designed to showcase patriarchal social structures deeply embedded in narrative forms. Through a variety of now well-documented techniques (her use of "playgiarism," hybrid forms, transgressive writing, among others), Acker's fictions trouble socio-political frameworks, demanding that readers question the discourses that shape and circumscribe their beliefs. It might be said that her work deliberately advances what David Castillo and Bill Eggington call "fictional awareness" in their book *Medialogies* (2016).

As Castillo writes in *Medialogies*,

> Our point is that fiction, art, philosophy have the power to infect our beliefs with the self-knowledge that keeps us from being enthralled by them, and with the self-difference that deflates the power of a rhetoric predicated on collapsing artifice and thing. Thus, what we could call a kind of "fictional awareness" lies at the heart of our approach to media...Fictional awareness, a reading skill honed by engaging in representations that reframe and problematize how the media frame and position reality, primes us to be critical receptors of media in general, and to be attuned to how our own identities and desires are implicated in mediatic representations.

While "fiction, art and philosophy," as they write, can similarly enhance a reader's "fictional awareness," I'd further argue that fiction—experimental fiction in particular—is ideally structured to "reframe and problematize" ordinary narratives by sensitizing readers to the subtle, often sophisticated, nuances of narrative gamesmanship which contours fiction into its wicked step-cousin forms: propaganda and lies.

In this light, fictional language might be viewed as a primer, even a kind of counter-messaging armature, for the language of alternate facts.

If experimental writing still has a role in the twenty-first century—the question at hand in this collection—given that literary reading according to the NEA is now at all time lows, it is precisely to present narratives which, by virtue of their variation, multiplicity, and difference, ask readers to idle in, digest, and analyze the stories they tell (or fail to tell, or tell incompletely) using a broad spectrum of *sui generis* techniques that require readers' engagement and self-aware intervention.

In other words, the interlocutive structure of experimental fiction—its call for an active reader (what Roland Barthes once described as a text's "writerly" characteristics)—presents readers with variable models for interrogating and puzzling out the narratives we regularly encounter, not just in novel forms, but on a daily basis in our media-saturated lives as well.

FRAMEWORDS

Paul West, 1991
"Much fiction is like mustard spread over the belly, take it or leave it, who cares. Some fiction has intentions on the reader and wants to inflict grievous bodily harm ....They create disturbances in the well-tempered harmony of everyday life."

Michael Riffaterre, 1990
"The only reason that the phrase fictional truth is not an oxymoron as 'fictitious truth' would be, is that fiction is a genre whereas lies are not. Being a genre it rests on conventions, of which the first and perhaps only one is that fiction specifically, but not always explicitly, excludes the intention to deceive. A novel always contains signs whose function is to remind readers that the tale they are being told is imaginary."

Lance Olsen, 2014
"So-called experimental fiction teaches a fundamental political lesson over and over again, as much through its structural complications as through its thematics: that the text of the text, the

text of our lives, and the text of the world can and should be other than they are."

DARPA, STORY ANALYSIS AND DECOMPOSING NARRATIVES

In 2011, DARPA (the Defense Advanced Research Projects Agency)—in effect, the high risk research wing of the US military, which invented both the internet and the hummingbird spy robot cam—announced a conference designed to investigate the specific role narrative plays "in security domains." The name of the workshop was: *Stories, Neuroscience and Experimental Technologies: Analysis and Decomposition of Narratives in Security Contexts.* In effect: STORyNET.

DARPA's hope for STORyNET was apparent: to develop technologies that could both detect propaganda (fiction), as well as design persuasive counter-messaging opportunities (more fiction).

The STORyNET conference announcement read as follows:

> Stories exert a powerful influence on human thoughts and behavior. They consolidate memory, shape emotions, cue heuristics and biases in judgment, influence in-group/out group distinctions, and may affect the fundamental contents of personal identity. It comes as no surprise that these influences make stories highly relevant to vexing security challenges such as radicalization, violent social mobilization, insurgency and terrorism, and conflict prevention and resolution. Therefore, understanding the role stories play in a security context is a matter of great import and some urgency. Ascertaining exactly what function stories enact, and by what mechanisms they do so, is a necessity if we are to effectively analyze the security phenomena shaped by stories. Doing this in a scientifically respectable manner requires a working theory of narratives, an understanding of what role narratives play in security

contexts, and examination of how to best analyze stories—decomposing them and their psychological impact systematically....To this end, the workshop will focus on surveying theories of narrative, understanding what role they play in security domains, and establishing the state of the art in story analysis and decomposition frameworks.

Mark Finlayson (author of "The Military Interest in Narrative" among other related articles) and one of the plenary speakers at the conference, discussed in his presentation on "Analogical Story Merging" how "security domains" might exploit fiction in real world contexts. For instance, in his PowerPoint presentation (briefly on-line after the STORyNET conference), he showed how stories from different genres like the Harry Potter and Star Wars series (fantasy and sci-fi respectively) might be reduced to the same graphed plot structure. He then demonstrated how the movements in five of Shakespeare's plays followed similar rises and falls in conflict. Finally, on a slide called "Plot Pattern Discovery," Finlayson made a leap from literary to real world contexts, graphing narratives of terrorism and malware attacks as similar trajectories of plot development.

Finlayson's implication was clear: all of these stories—from Shakespeare to sci-fi to the Stuxnet crisis—can be reduced to their expressions of plot. His next point, implied if not embedded on a Powerpoint slide, soon became evident: if readers understand a fictional narrative's movement, they might also understand, *even predict*, through "Analogical Story Merging" the movement of "plots" in their own cultures. Institutions might then plausibly "decompose" narrative plot points in developing crises in order to derive desirable narrative endings for their "security domains."

It should go without saying that this theory fails to take into account the role that language plays in fiction. Fiction is never, simply, an expression of plot.

More crucially for the purposes of this argument, however, Finlayson's remarks reveal an astonishing turn in literary criticism:

the most common, idiomatically expressed beliefs about fiction—for instance, "Truth is stranger than fiction" or "Fiction reveals truths that reality obscures"—have, in the twenty-first century, begun to decompose.

If, conventionally, fiction has exploited the realm of fact for its purposes, it's not too much to say that, now, the realm of fact has begun to exploit fiction.

Put another way: fiction, once viewed primarily as entertainment, is now being deployed as a tool, even a weapon, for real world ends.

As one researcher familiar with the DARPA initiative reported to *Wired* in 2011: "The government is already trying to control the message, so why not have the science to do it in a systematic way?"

FRAMEWORDS

Ronald Reagan, 2004
"Trees cause more pollution than automobiles do."

New York Department of Environmental Conservation
There is "no record of any documented instance of groundwater contamination caused by hydraulic fracturing for gas well development in New York, despite the use of this technology in thousands of wells across the state during the past 50 or more years."

Sweetsurprise.com (2012)
"High fructose corn syrup is made from corn, a natural grain product and is a natural sweetener. High fructose corn syrup contains no artificial or synthetic ingredients or color additives. It also meets the U.S. Food and Drug Administration's requirements for use of the term 'natural.'"

GIVE FICTION CREDIT—THE ETYMOLOGY AND ECONOMY OF BELIEF: A CONCLUSION

The concept of "fiction" in Western culture originates from the Latin root *fingere*: to shape, to form, to devise. To sculpt as out of clay.

In other words, fiction arises as an act, an operation: a muscular engagement of shaping worlds from words. A participatory process of accumulation and decay that constructs a credible world with—alongside of—a reader.

Credibility, too, has a crucial Latinate origin in *credere*—to believe, to confide, to entrust—which now gives us the word "credit." Put another way? Credibility in fiction is always a two way street. A literary economy that fiction facilitates.

Fiction, in short, might be said to be founded as a form of exchange, a loan: words given and returned, perhaps even amplified, with interest.

If experimental writing, specifically, can be said to do one thing (given its distinctive variations) it is showcasing the "decomposition" of the fictional act itself: revealing for readers the discourses, the languages, the bodies on which stories are built, while encouraging a self-reflective engagement from readers about how their own stories have been built from the discourses, the languages, and the bodies around them.

The question, even now, isn't *whether* we're reading truth or fiction.

The issue—the site of resistance that experimental fiction continues to facilitate through its decomposed forms—is exposing how discourses of truth or fiction are shaped so that self-reflective readers can best judge what they are reading themselves.

FRAMEWORDS

Donald Trump, 2017
"A great and important day at the United Nations. Met with leaders of many nations who agree with much (or all) of what I stated in my speech!"

Sean Spicer, 2017
"Our intention is never to lie to you."

Nikki Haley, 2017
"None of us want war."

23

Experimental Reading
Warren Motte

It is undoubtedly true that the will to innovate can be identified in almost any literary text at almost any time, and it is equally true that certain texts display that feature far more prominently than others, quite regardless of period. Nevertheless, the notion of "experimental writing" as a recognizable and *systematic* literary tendency is doubtless a construction of our own time. Though I realize all of a sudden that the term "our own time," which I use so blithely, also demands further nuance, for it, too, can be understood in several different ways. So to be more precise about it, allow me to suggest that experimental writing (from which I shall now remove those pernicious quotation marks) is an emanation of the literary avant-garde. In the French tradition (which is the one I know best, and the one I will mostly cite in what follows), the rise of the avant-garde is a matter of debate. Some people see its birth in Baudelaire; others contend that Mallarmé inaugurates it; still, others point toward Dada and Surrealism, two decades into the twentieth century. I have always thought that 1896 is a pleasing date because it was in that year that Alfred Jarry's *Ubu roi* was first performed, with such astonishing results. One will recall that there were fistfights and full-blown melees in the theater itself and that William Butler Yeats expressed his own bewildered reaction in five pithy words: "After us, the Savage God." Beginning with the magnificent solecism "Merdre!," *Ubu roi* retains its power to shock a century after its appearance—and how many cultural artifacts of any sort can claim that distinction? Indeed, it was not until 2009 that the play was admitted into the hallowed repertory of the Comédie Française.

The power to shock, the iconoclastic impulse, the resistance to recuperation, the obdurate and aggressive rejection of the old in favor of the new: all of these are hallmarks of the nascent avant-garde. They find expression in texts as otherwise dissimilar as Raymond Roussel's *Impressions d'Afrique* (1910), Guillaume Apollinaire's *Calligrammes* (1918), Tristan Tzara's *Manifeste dada* (1918), and André Breton's *Manifeste du surréalisme* (1924). One other feature that gradually becomes apparent as the avant-garde launches itself onto the cultural horizon and gathers a good head of steam is the impulse toward systematic experimentation, or, in other terms, an organized and programmatic process targeting specific goals.

One of those goals points directly and inevitably to *us*, as readers and consumers of literary culture. More precisely stated, the experimental text *involves* us, enrolling us willingly or unwillingly in the process of textual production, and enfranchising us in that process as full partners. In the first instance, it may shock and bewilder us insofar as it beggars traditional, normative strategies of reading and interpretation. Yet by the same token, it grabs us and demands a reaction from us; it engages us and insists that we *do* something with it; it rejects outright a passive reception in favor of an active, articulative one. Briefly stated, it makes us part of the deal whether we wish (and *seek*) to be enlisted, or not. It brings me moreover, conveniently if not subtly, to the proposition that lies at the heart of my argument:

Experimental writing obliges us to read experimentally.

For in point of fact, we can read it no other way. We grope around the experimental text, seeking points of ingress. We test this strategy of reading, then that one, in order to make sense of the thing. We try this interpretation on for size, then reject it in favor of another that promises to make more sense. We go at the experimental text hammer and tongs, gradually realizing that the text has been conceived with that very process in mind, and that in fact it *anticipates* our interpretive efforts. In other words, whatever else the experimental text may speak about—a young man coming of age in Dublin, for instance; or the difficulty of waiting for a person named "Godot" who never arrives; or the fact that the letter

E has disappeared from the alphabet—it also (and crucially) speaks about *us*, and about our efforts to come to terms with it. Moreover, it addresses that speech directly to us, in an unmediated manner— just as if it were inviting us to engage in a conversation, a conversation that is potentially infinite in its dimensions, as Maurice Blanchot has pointed out.

In order to illustrate my contention more precisely, allow me to call upon a moment in Jean-Philippe Toussaint's *The Bathroom*, a quirky and wonderfully idiosyncratic novel published in 1985. It occurs when his protagonist is gazing out of his window into the rainswept streets of Paris, and it goes like this:

> It was raining. The street was wet, the sidewalks dark. Cars were parking. Other cars, already parked, were covered with rain. People were crossing the street quickly, going in and out of the post office in the modern building across from me. A little vapor began to cover my windowpane. Behind the thin coat of mist, I observed the passersby sending their letters. The rain gave them a conspiratorial air: stopping in front of the mailbox, they would draw an envelope from their coat and thrust it through the slot very quickly so as not to get it wet, meanwhile pulling up their collars against the rain. I put my face close to the window and, eyes against the glass, suddenly had the impression that all these people were inside an aquarium. Perhaps they were afraid? The aquarium was slowly filling.

The narrator's position is a curious one if one stops to examine it closely. On the one hand, he is inside his apartment, gazing out at the street. But it occurs to him by fancy that the people outside are actually in an aquarium, and that notion puts him, virtually at least, in a rather different position, that of someone outside gazing in. Which perspective trumps the other, the literal or the figural, the rational or the fanciful, the pragmatic or the aesthetic? Is it possible to inhabit both sites simultaneously? Or can we imagine him oscillating between one and the other, attentive to both perspectives, learning the lessons that both put on offer, deciphering the world he inhabits doubly, rather than singly?

Not to put too fine a point on it, I am convinced that this

passage contains a parable. A parable of writing and artistic creation, certainly, because it is clear that Toussaint is speaking about imagination, and the way it can transform the most ordinary event into one worthy of narrative interest. Yet I believe that he is also speaking about reading here because what is his protagonist doing, other than *reading* the street scene before him, as it is inscribed on the virtual page of the rainy window? If such is the case, what might this passage have to say about reading and about readers? One idea it puts forward involves readerly mobility: it suggests that reading is fundamentally dynamic and that readers are neither definitively inside or outside, but rather inside-out and outside-in as it were, turn and turn about. That notion, which seems so scandalously metaleptic, is actually a venerable one which one can trace back to Aristotle's theory of *catharsis*, should one feel compelled to do so. I am *not* Oedipus the King, his problems are *not* mine, I *neither* killed my father *nor* slept with my mother—yet that does not prevent me from suffering right along with him for the space of two hours.

Examining the stances that we adopt as readers more critically than we usually think about them, it becomes clear that many dimensions of our readerly behavior are a bit more fluid than we might have imagined them to be. When we read, we are neither subject nor object exclusively, for instance, but instead both subject and object in turn. Phenomenal worlds and textual worlds are never absolutely distinct, and we stride from one into the other as a matter of course. Imagination lavishly informs our experience of the real while experience of the real necessarily structures our imagination—and it would be a real shame if such were not the case. Our position, in other terms, is much like that of the writer, since we are always both *in* and *out*. The experimental text underscores that analogy heavily and plays upon it for effect, reminding us insistently of the collaborative, articulative character of literature, and constantly urging us to play our part therein. The incessant mobility that it demands of us can seem like a curse at times, to be sure; but at others we may see it as a matter of privilege and favor. For my own part, I am persuaded that the way we are both *here* and *there* in literature constitutes one of the most reliable sources of a deep and abiding readerly pleasure.

24
This Is Not a Pipe Dream
Doug Nufer

As someone who writes by using formal constraints,[1] I often find myself wondering what I have written. Is it poetry or prose? Will it go the distance to become a book or run its course in a few pages? A distinguishing attribute of experimental literature is how it challenges traditional genres and classifications. The form of an experimental work is not to be taken for granted or by default, but must be open to reinvention, so that the standards that define what makes something a poem or story must be questioned and made to serve the topic. In the process of doing this, it's not uncommon for writers to make work that defies classification, eludes easy categorization, or lays claim to literary territory that may seem preposterous.

Why bother? Grant givers, publishers, and reviewers typically require some sort of tag to sort out the writing they would award, publish, or review, however absurd such a branding exercise may be. Various tactics to deal with categorizing form and genre come into play, some of them useful. Harry Mathews puts *Selected Declarations of Dependence* (1977), his book of prose

---

[1] Nicholson Baker, Raymond Roussel, Nabokov, and many others have mastered the use of footnotes, so it's hardly experimental for me to join the party now, but what the hell? I thought of deploying Roussel's *New Impressions of Africa* (1932) multiple parentheses (which I've also used), and Raymond Queneau's *Exercises in Style* (1947) model of a cavalcade of constraints (which Louis Bury recently did quite well in *Exercises in Criticism* [2015]), as well as other tributes to formal manipulation, but the footnote gambit not only seems most useful but also a handy repository to dispense with information and remarks that would otherwise clutter the text.

and poetry made from split and recombined proverbs he calls perverbs, in the category "Miscellanies." How is Samuel Beckett's *How It Is* (*Comment c'est*, 1961), with its prose lines without periods,[2] a novel rather than a prose poem? If Gertrude Stein anticipates the cottage industry of creative writing manuals with her title *How to Write* (1931), David Markson taunts literary taxonomists by using *This Is Not a Novel* (2001) to call a novel made up of a collection of quotes from and impressions of books he had read. To the question of branding, I'll appropriate an answer Lance Olsen posed at the end of a reading at Powell's Books in Portland to the question of why anyone would write experimental literature, "Because it's fun."

Nobody seems to have as much fun at the classification game as purveyors of conceptual poetry. To cite a few heavyweights, Robert Fitterman repackages the lyrics of the Nirvana album *Nevermind* (1991) as an eponymous 700-page conceptual poem, Kenneth Goldsmith amasses a similar bulk to reproduce one issue of *The New York Times* as a conceptual poem in the form of the book *Day*, and Vanessa Place, in a way, outslugs everybody by re-contextualizing not the works of others but the legal depositions from her day job as an appellate attorney to make the three volume conceptual poem, *Tragodia*, beginning with volume 1, *Statement of Facts* (2010).[3] While some if not most people might scoff at the strategy of passing off such verbiage as "poetry," I sometimes if not mostly read poems that are really prose set in line breaks, after being guided in my reading apostasy by Marjorie Perloff, who went over the works of various prize-winning poets by doing just that to their lines.[4]

Back to the beginning, there is the constraint, the notion of trying some procedure, rule, or set of rules to make a composition.

---

[2] And how is it that some renderings of *How It Is* (1961) that I read online supply periods where Beckett did not put them in his original French edition and his translation into English?

[3] Blanc Press in Los Angles issued the first volume in 2010 and the others are forthcoming.

[4] I couldn't remember whether she or Charles Bernstein wrote this essay, so I asked each of them. He said he thought that sounded like her work and she thought it might be from *Georgia Review 35*, Winter, 1981, pp. 855-69: "The Linear Fallacy."

This can take years to end in mush or it can find its form immediately. Before I had the title *Lifeline Rule* for a novel I'd just begun, of alternating consonants and vowels,[5] I made a list of authors whose names are spelled that way, in order to ask them to write blurbs by using that constraint.[6] More often, I arrive at form after flailing around in the doldrums of indecision. I envy Kim Rosenfield for taking the shows that Bob Hope put on for the armed services as a prompt for *USO: I'll Be Seeing You* (2013), and Mónica de la Torre for lighting upon an office furniture vision of a job fair inspired by Nature Theater of Oklahoma's treatment of Kafka's *Amerika* (1927) to conceive of *The Happy End/ All Welcome* (2017). Not that Nabokov's *Pale Fire* (1962) wrote itself, but brilliant ideas and flawless execution have a way of seeming to make art magically materialize. As for my projects in search of the right form, I think that the novel is the ultimate constraint for difficulty but that poetry lends itself better to the most demanding constraints. That is to say, anybody can write a poem without the letter e, but Georges Perec's *La Disparition* (*A Void*, 1969) is the ultimate lipogram novel, if not the ultimate novel driven by any constraint; and Christian Bök took the lipogram's cousin, univocality, to limits beyond the limits of the novel in the one-vowel-per-section prose poetry of *Eunoia* (2001). From the Oulipian constraint of embedded words, I played with strings of letters that repeated to form different words. For longer than it should have taken me to realize, these phrases were lines, not sentences, and *The Me Theme* would be poetry,[7] not prose.

This attention to (or, obsession with) form is important for all writers, as is the relationship between form and content.[8] Terms

---

[5] The constraint is called "conovowel," devised by William Gillespie. The novel was published by Spuyten Duyvil in 2015.

[6] Hey, Carole Maso, did you ever get my email?

[7] Published by Sagging Meniscus Press in 2017. I wonder what the standard is about bibliographical attribution, now that so many book reviews omit the names of publishers, as if we're all just supposed to look online and buy from Amazon.

[8] Gilbert Sorrentino described himself as a writer "who has always been convinced that form is actually and inevitably content, that the novel's ideas are inextricable from the novel's structure, and that the novel reveals, ultimately, the novelist," in my article "No End to Trying: Gilbert Sorrentino's Novel

like "avant-garde" and "innovative" may be beside the point, although "experimental" gets bonus points for irritating the piss out of a lot of people, even people who write and publish experimental literature.

Some years ago, to get away from all of that and more, I took to riding my bicycle for hours along the rivers south of Seattle. Sure enough, towns sprang to life as characters in a crime novel scenario that had to be composed as a poem, or else it would be forgotten. The need to memorize hatched one of the constraining principles of the composition: doubles. Rhymes (writing/riding; waiting/wading), eye rhymes (number as in integer or as in with less sensitivity), and names that stood for characters and places at the same time led the way. The interchangeable nature of rhymes made for a reliance on duplicity and ambiguity, which resonated in the title: *The Dammed*, even if most people would hear it as *The Damned*. This brought another dilemma: the primary expression of a text built on the duplicity of sounds must be performance. Any written version, whether labeled as poetry or prose, would be essentially no more than a score or script. What kind of performance? Poetry recital? Recording? Movie? Play? All of the above? I didn't care whether any of this was experimental, innovative, or whatever; I didn't particularly care to come up with just the right form or genre to put it across. The unmoored nature of its niche was a relief. Moreover, there was no need to settle for one form and dump the others, although it was tempting to apply Marcel Bénabou's advice to readers to my role as writer: Dump this book while you still can. Instead, I heeded the hedonist call of an old beer commercial: Who says you can't have it all?

I wrote it as a poem, memorized and performed parts and eventually all of it. After the poem came a script for a movie, a movie by Amy Billharz that became a backdrop for a multimedia stage show.[9] Taking a cue from my conceptual poetry friends, or

Novels," in *The Stranger*, Oct. 19, 2000, which took five years to get from acceptance to publication, and all the while Sorrentino kept writing more books so that I had to keep revising.

[9] A week before an exhibition and full performance of *The Dammed* was to take place at the Hedreen Gallery at Seattle University, the show was cancelled by the curator, who had been told by the drama department that we couldn't have

from F. Scott Fitzgerald, who wrote *The Great Gatsby* (1925) in blank verse,[10] I revised *The Dammed* as prose for *The Brooklyn Rail* fiction section. It was a better story than any I had on hand or wanted to write, and I didn't want to send an excerpt of a novel. I wrote the story version from memory, leaving out one line deliberately and another by mistake, in what turned out to be an adventure in formatting and punctuation. After it ran in the *Rail*, it entered (and lost) a storytelling contest put on by sticklers for generic propriety that called for prose. Meanwhile, an earlier version of the poem has been up for years on ubuweb in its "Publishing the Unpublishable" series, a short segment of it is on Vimeo, I still perform parts or all of it, and the full movie version to accompany a live performance lurks on file if the occasion comes.[11]

---

a live show in the art gallery then because they had another event scheduled in the theater next door, so we did a cramped version of the show at the Canoe Club, a few blocks away. As frustrating as this was, it was a bit of a relief not to pay for musicians and the video documentation that would be a step toward getting the show on stage elsewhere; and, after all, the indeterminate nature of the show's manifestation was in keeping with the shifting nature of the composition, form, and genre of *The Dammed*, and the fate of its premiere was practically a foregone conclusion for something that sounded like *The Damned*.

[10] "And SO we BEAT on, BOATS aGAINST the CUR-/rent, BORNE back CEASElessLY inTO the PAST," I said when poet and bookstore owner John Marshall told me this. Some professor mentioned it to him, as if it were common knowledge.

[11] After we first exchanged letters (real letters, not email), I occasionally wrote to Gilbert Sorrentino and he would reply. One time I sent him a poem I was working on, made up entirely of the punch lines of Borscht Belt jokes, "What Was, Was." He wrote back a letter consisting entirely of punch lines from other Borscht Belt jokes. All but one of them I had come across in my research through encyclopedias of Jewish humor: "Yingle, yingle." Nobody I asked had heard of it. Before I asked him for the rest of the joke, he died. What was, was.

25

Problematics of the First Page as a Way of Being
Lance Olsen

what is a first page?
Once upon a time, Martin Buber recounts in *Tales of the Hasidim*, one of Rabbi Levi Yitzchak of Berditchev's students asked him why the first page number is missing in all the tractates of the Babylonian Talmud. "However much a man may learn," the rabbi replied, "he should always remember that he has not even gotten to the first page."

what is *neuland*?
What I want to say is that for so-called experimental writing practices, reading is a problem. Reading is *the* problem. We know we are in an example of it because without warning we sense we are always already on our way to a first page that will never present itself. We feel the need to invent a new language, a new set of coordinates, to describe and discuss where we have discovered ourselves. German has a word that approximates the feeling I'm after: *Neuland* —new territory, unfamiliar space, uncharted waters, unexplored terrain. *Ich kenne mich das noch nicht aus. Das ist Neuland für mich.* I don't know my way around here. That's a new country for me.

what is reading?

What I want to say is that so-called experimental writing practices have less to do with *what* we are reading than with *how*. A two-name shorthand for this: *Barthes* + *Derrida*. They exemplify modes of deliberate self-reflexive misreading, over-reading, slant-rhyme reading, hyper-idiosyncratic associative reading that through one optic reveals a puckish parody of New Criticism's earnest emphasis on close reading backed by a (naïve) belief that a work of literature functions as a self-contained aesthetic object. They simultaneously stand for an awareness that texts don't exist in any meaningful way until the event of reading occurs, and that that event is less dependent on the text itself than on the quality of mind of the reader that engages with it. Anyone, that is, can attempt to read Balzac's brief novella "Sarrasine." Barthes's circus of the mind in motion as evinced in *S/Z*, however, can take for granted in its encounter that all theory is spiritual autobiography and go on to (mis)mine Balzac's work into an explosively illuminating instant about, well, Barthes's imagination. Anyone can attempt reading Hegel and/or Genet. Derrida's circus of the mind in motion as evinced in *Glas*, however, understands it can understand philosopher and author only by (mis)eventing and (re)inventing them, denarrating them into material metaphors that turn text into performance art. Every page of Barthes's and

Derrida's projects becomes a reminder that we have yet to reach the first.

what is a beginning?

"Forgive me for all this philosophy," Matthew Goulish apologizes in *39 Microlectures: In Proximity of Performance*, "but what I'm trying to say is, in reaching the end of our road of beginnings, we now realize that beginnings are all there are."

what are my eyes?

My eyes are never my eyes. They are my eyes. They are not not my eyes. How they read depends on my own imagination, education, age, where I live, socioeconomic context, gender, race, awareness of my body, comprehension of language structures and functions, what interpretive communities I intuit myself part of, how I have complicated those terms, how those terms have complicated me, how many times I have encountered a particular text and how many times I have unlearned to see it, how many times I have been in love, how many things and people and ideas and hopes I have lost, how many I have gained, how deeply I have experienced hurt and hope, how much I am capable of feeling, how much I am capable of thinking, how many family resemblances I can constellate between the text at hand and those I have previously read, my relationship to the other arts, to politics, to the world of accidents, my transactions with other beings, other things, and so forth, as well as where I am positioned in history with respect to that text.

what is time?

Another way of saying this: One cannot read *Tristram Shandy* as Sterne wrote it or his contemporaries read and understood it. One can't even quite know what that last sentence means. One can only read Sterne's astonishment through, say, Joyce's *Ulysses* already having been in the universe, Beckett's *Unnamable,* Carson's *Nox*—whether or not, of course, one has ever actually read those novels or not. One can only read, in other words, through one's now, however one might begin to grasp and perplex that bewildering noun.

what is now?

The real question for writers, I suggest to my graduate students in my seminars on and within experimental writing practices, is this: *How do we write the contemporary in a way that doesn't simply perpetuate the past ... and yet (mis)understands, consumes, and thinks through it? How do we beyond yesterday when "beyond" exists solely as a transitive verb? How do we create possibility spaces in which everything can be mindfully tried, challenged, undone, rethought, and failed in productive, incandescent gestures for a purpose—even if that purpose remains a mystery to us?*

what is a political heterodoxy?

While each of us will answer those questions radically and fruitfully differently from each other and—depending on where we are and when in our lives—even from our selves, every answer will propose by its presence that we can and should envision the text of the text, the text of our lives, and the text of the world other than they are, and thus contemplate the idea of fundamental change in all three.

what is reading?

Goulish again: "For each word read brings to an end the life of the reader who has not read the book, ushering in the life of the reader who has."

what is a first page?

A first page, then, is the composite of words you are just about to reach, yet haven't, and never will. Traveling toward it becomes a rich exercise both in unknowing and almosting.

what is slow thinking?

One difference between art and entertainment has to do with the speed of perception. Art willfully slows and complicates reading, hearing, and/or viewing so we are challenged to re-think and re-feel form and experience. Entertainment, on the other hand, willfully accelerates and simplifies reading, hearing, and/or viewing so that we don't have to think about or feel very much of anything at all except, perhaps, the adrenalin rush of the spectacle in front of us. So-called experimental writing practices is a method of art intensified, pointedly made more difficult, in order to create what Renee Gladman calls a Thinking Text—although perhaps closer to what I'm getting at would be a Thinkfeeling Text.

what is thinkfeeling?

Question: Can a piece of entertainment be read as a piece of art? Answer: cultural studies.

what is a political heterodoxy?
Robert Haas: "We pass these things on, / probably, because we are what we can imagine."

what is contemporary?
[[Once upon a time, we knew all this. I wonder when and why we began to forget.]] Donald Barthelme: "Art is not difficult because it wishes to be difficult, but because it wishes to be art. However much the writer might long to be, in his work, simple, honest, and straightforward, these virtues are no longer available to him. He discovers that in being simple, honest, and straightforward, nothing much happens: he speaks the speakable, whereas what we are looking for is the as-yet unspeakable, the as-yet unspoken."

what is thinkfeeling?
Question: Does cultural studies unknowingly *embrace and maintain the very globalized* corporate culture that it claims to critique by means of its reading strategies that, as Curtis White maintains, tend to eschew close, rigorous engagement with the page in order to search texts "for symptoms supporting the sociopolitical or theoretical template of the critic"? Answer: ————

what is reading?
N. Katharine Hayles makes what I find a tremendously helpful distinction between two cognitive modes, *deep attention* and *hyper attention*. Deep attention, usually associated with normative writing and reading, is the sort able to concentrate on a single object thoroughly for an extended period of time. Think of your experience reading a novel by, say, Dostoevsky.

Hyper attention, on the other hand, switches focus rapidly and often. It is attention with the jitters. Think of your experience navigating a video game like, say, *Berserk and the Band of the Hawk*. Oddly, so-called experimental writing practices often invite you to employ both cognitive modes at the same time: an intense, extended focus coupled with a quick-scanning function in order to discern both the deep-structure rules and limits of serious play. Another way of saying this: Who are "we" now, and now, and now, and how, and why?

what is slow thinkfeeling?

To slow thinkfeel a text is to begin to raise elemental questions that otherwise remain invisible about reading: *Where does a book exist? In what ways does how a page matters matter? How do we read with our hands? Our legs? How is the ideology of characterization not a psychological but sociocultural activity? How is reading the opposite of a fixed habit? How could the same be said about so-called experimental writing practices? How could it not?* All of which is to announce the obvious: so-called experimental writing practices don't comprise a laundry list of techniques, the wheel continuously reinventing itself, the flavor of the week, but rather a way of being in the world that foregrounds radical curiosity, heresy, contemplation, complication, fluidity, adaptability, risk, heterogeneity, acute presence, a natural rebelliousness against death in all its manifestations, unpredictability, unfamiliarity, astonishment, disruption, self-consciousness, passionate analytical thinkfeeling, contention, shock, resistance, joyful failure, pleasure, process instead of product, reading as a kind of writing, writing as a kind of reading, literate rather than fiscal economies, collective ecologies instead of competitive ones, the replacement of the Romantic myth of the gifted solitary artist with rhizomatic interrelationships of support, social arrangements based on loose affiliations rather than standardized hierarchies, robust independent literary activism as the dominant means of production and dissemination.

what is a future?
The science fiction genre appears to be a test in prediction, an intellectual tool to help us think about tomorrow. How right did William Gibson get cyberspace, H.G. Wells time travel? Nearer the case, naturally, is that SF's deep lesson, over and over again, is that tomorrow will forever remain unknowable, unspeakable. To ask what so-called experimental writing practices will look like next week, next year, in two decades, is a non-question, a grammatical mistake masquerading as inquiry, a fool's game—and one, obviously, that's very difficult not to want to play.

what is a future?
I'm interested instead in how certain questions will continue to be answered elliptically, giving rise to a more complex and generative set of questions. How, I wonder, for instance, will the formulation of selfhood and its manifestations in so-called experimental writing practices be posed, unlearned, and relearned, rethought, and what will that tell us about who "we" are becoming (that pronoun yet another grammatical mistake deployed as a metaphysics)? How will the development of various technologies continue to trouble our notions of narrativity and the book in enriching ways? As the book continues to dematerialize into Kindles and iPads, how will the

proliferation of book arts push back, reasserting the materiality of the page, the event of reading, while challenging the outdated idea that quantity somehow equals quality? How can so-called experimental writing practices beyond Young-Hae Chang and Heavy Industries' film texts, Christian Bök's xenotexts, or Shelley Jackson's skin project—or is that in some way essentially the wrong question to advance, or the wrong way to advance it?

what is a novel?
With respect to my own work, I'm equally interested in investigating what the so-called experimental novel—what all novels, really, if to varying degrees—can do and will continue to be able to do that other genres can't and won't: extended explorations of deep consciousness and language. In other words: how will the novel both persist in being itself (a form that historically has never understood its form) and always already almost something else?

what is a first page?
I don't know. You don't know. Nobody does. That's why we're faithfully, unfaithfully, futilely, gratefully, vitally, painfully, provisionally, clumsily, determinedly, joyfully undoing what we do.

what is a first page?
...

26

Monkey Business (towards aping literature)
Vanessa Place and Naomi Toth

In any event, as an event, we see this sort of thing as of no more or less significance than a reply to an email containing a video of instant coffee and milk on shelves of a supermarket with no caption.

On the subject of naming, what do you say to "collaborator"? For production is guilt-making by virtue of creation. Palpable, but not pronounced, the fantasy thereby traversed. Our goal being the shock of the moment when you see you've said more than you knew, for writing is stain-making, and has always been, and so this will be too, inevitably.

Like a barrelful of monkeys.

Point of presumption: we don't believe in a *dehors*. Or only a *dehors* that is the flip side of a *dedans*, that encloses nothing therefore. The matter being neither within nor without. Only the remainder is what counts, the too much and the not enough, the more and the less, which makes more or less enough, perhaps, to go on.

Monkey-making; e.g., this report to an academy.

Assuming literature heretofore is a play staged by man, we propose monkeys. Monkeys running barefaced and backwards, because there is no real human flight but from the present, and no greater human hope than the hope that there is no unconscious, after all.

Ergo: to write a monkey-passion play, conviction set in reverse:

Resurrection (the pardon, when man becomes monkey), followed by execution (the sentence of having to be merely man, not monkey), then trial (what greater crime is there, what more brutal accusation, than "merely man"), and finally, last supper or betrayal (a cannibalistic invitation to partake of the host, to dissect the one now strutting on stage). Here is our body, take and know.

Ending with a question: is murder violent enough to appease if there is no pain, if there is no soul anymore?

Or less.

Note that this is not the question of the god-forsaken man, but of the one who knows neither man's convictions, nor his pardons.

Raising another hope by way of a question: what is it that allows one to look at another and say you are close enough for me to judge and different enough for me to kill?

Note: monkeys will not stand for an autopsy of another monkey, making them the better man.

As a story, the reversed resurrection story is not bad at all, or just bad enough for us:
No to straight reversal or dumb père-version, the sacreligion of the teenager who deep down still loves daddy.[1] No to a relay in which the opposition of divine versus human is simply shifted along a tack, transposed for endless replay, a man in a monkey-suit. No to making of the monkey nothing but a metaphor.

---

[1] Jacques Lacan on James Joyce, in *Le Sinthome* (1975-76): "*L'imagination d'être le rédempteur, dans notre tradition au moins, est le prototype de ce que, ce n'est pas pour rien que je l'écrive :* la père-version. *C'est dans la mesure où il y a rapport de fils à père, et ceci depuis très longtemps, qu'a surgi l'idée loufoque du rédempteur.*"

The trick is to keep monkey monkey.

But that's quite a trick.[2]

Like a medieval painting: the thing is the thing, as well as a vignette along some castle corridor, simultaneous goings on, a tautological allegory, tapped out in time. The animal *as such* is absent. Because the monkey never existed as a subject of discourse, only ever as discourse's uncontainable object.

So what we want is the simultaneous with a bit of denouement, the metallic taste of showbiz, the flash of a circus, and the comfort of a cage. That denouement (the show-stopper) being the judge of us, the shard of mirror serving to pop the protection of the performance as such, that why-am-I-here which sticks in the moment of desire—as illusion, or article of faith.

I.e., the immanent subjective, because that's the final cannibalism, isn't it? The same problem of context with only the thinnest text. Like our supermarket video, and your latest poems. Judgement inevitably falls, like a mirror, the reflection sending back more than we thought we were displaying. Showing the want of judgment itself, lovely and unbearable, coupled with the satisfaction of a good shatter. People like mirrors. And seven year's bad luck is at least something you can count on.

When monkeys look into mirrors, they first examine their genitals.

Like desire, the will, want, and wish to be seen, always too much yet never enough, and as the cliché knows, every good confession accompanies an execution, and vice versa.

Although when monkeying about, confession becomes execution, and vice versa.

---

[2] *Contra,* the therianthropic/theanthropic fantasy of originality.

Just as Kafka's ape mutilates his monkey to make his man, and vice versa. Aping literature is all writing can do: reflect the monkey's act back to his monkey self, rehearsing and replaying the scene of the academy's listening. More, for you.[3] More to be *read*. Like a sign that says, "Exit" in red.

Red for Rotpeter's cheek, for reading, for branded sheep, and a slash of raspberry, as on *just* desserts. Red for the mark of Cain, the sign of the son's banishment from the Father's presence, the signature murder; the birthmark, then, of the human as such. The scar you other monkeys groom so prettily, its braid a noose for the next generation.

Crime, here, is the inaugural act of the artist. Manifesting guilt while preserving life. Life as punishment, a punishment which will never be enough.

Champagne?

Monkeys make man make monkey faces at man, and only the monkey takes offense.

In this monkey business, thingness must be sensed everywhere. The work comes whole and incarnate, and preferably life-sized— a host appetizing enough to attract and to evoke disgust at satiation. This is the cannibalistic curse of history, and the rounding satisfaction of desire, in the sense of *when will we have our fill* and *why can't I ever have mine?*

Point of presumption: *mine* is by birthright, *i.e.*, by way of my desire.

Yes to champagne, darling, of course.

---

[3] "*By day I cannot bear to see her, for she has the crazed, bewildered look of the trained animal in her eye, no one else sees it but I, and I can't bear it. Besides, I am not appealing for any man's verdict, I am only imparting knowledge, I am only making a report. To you, honoured Members of the Academy, I have only made a report.*"

Self-execution as self-judgment. In our aping literature, the daily populace goes about their daily business, believing they are who they imagine themselves to be, while we two thieves (there are always two) stand at two corners of the stage making confessions about faith: the opposite of identity, or art, or even performance, which so often amount to the same thing.

Knowing that all confessions are excruciating, going, as they do, from tongue to ear, ear to tongue, a feast of sacrificial parts and sublimated flesh like so many ladies and their edible little fingers. As harrowing as any hope.

For if it's not a bit unbearable, then it's barely worth doing.

More champagne?

The ancients, apparently, only ever referred to the body as whole when it was a corpse, the living body giving itself up in parts only. And redeeming itself *idem*, as infinity inheres only in bits.

Monkey see, monkey do.

Yes to heart-shaped chocolates, yes to the inconsequence of desire, yes to the reading of every autopsy report from the head of every dinner table, done as prayerfully as when we confess ourselves to our personal screens to make and touch digital beings in whom we trust, in whom we may be forgiven, and not forgotten. The confessional gate is wide and the road broad, for it does not lead to heaven.

But it is a gesture of monkey love.

For what we love, when we love, is the empty report. Speech that has no real communication, or no communication that counts *for* anything, as its goal. To say something and have something else heard, including the grain of the saying. The smallest friction of sound, finally.

Speak softly, catch monkey.

Which is the job of the Hostess. Insult the guest by making them feel special. As if they were not part of a system of exchange. As if they were frictionless, consumed, yet inconsummate.

Enter Rotpeter's chimp: the silent "she" blankly refusing to play, erasing any self that obtrudes too much into the field of vision while setting the scene for the serious game of knowledge. (Note here that there are always three, not two.)

Chimp and Hostess: each sweet and terrifying by turns, necessary solaces and seemingly superfluous frames, neither directly addressed nor entirely evacuated, the only ones to hear and see certain monkey bites. Who speak, even silently, an imperative evil. And, dearest, as our collaborator, you must tell us what you want. Don't worry if it's nothing special.[4]

Remember that gods don't look in mirrors, and genitals—*as such*—are the measure of man.

Tous punctum, sans point.

We are nothing if not unremarkable.

Because monkeys know to just type it out and send it off and leave some self hanging in suspense ... *et voilà*, the noose returns, just in time for the sentence, the lead line of literature's own autopsy report, that monkey-wrench which serves as our weapon and our crime—aping literature.

Leaving you, the chimp on the other side, alone on stage, still, and unmasked.

---

[4] Roland Barthes, in *Mythologies* (1957): "*Et c'est une duplicité propre au spectacle bourgeoise: entre le signe intellectuel et le signe viscéral, cet art dispose hypocritement un signe bâtard, à la fois elliptique et prétentieux, qu'il baptise du nom pompeux de 'naturel.'*"

27

Experimental Criticism
Gerald Prince

In spite, or perhaps because of, its long life, experimental writing continues to flourish. It is a vast territory many of whose parts lie open to more exploration and elaboration. Even in a much cultivated area like fiction, a good number of possibilities are still unexploited or underexploited. Indeed, narratology, which aims to account for what all and only narratives have in common and for what allows them to be different *qua* narratives, functions as a powerful rhetoric by pointing to unrealized narrative potentialities. For example, novels could consist of free direct discourses (or streams of consciousness) issuing not only from single individuals or consciousnesses but also from (more or less) heterogeneous groups or collectivities, from plurivocal "we's" instead of monovocal "I's." They could feature multi-voiced rather than merely dual-voiced free indirect discourses, mixing several language situations rather than only two. They could utilize all known forms of point of view successively: standard types of perspective (i.e, zero-degree, internal, and external), of course, but also hypothetical viewpoints or more eccentric cases like compound, unspecified, undecidable, or split point of view. They could be multipersoned, adopting in turn singular and plural first, second, and third person narration, and using I and we, thou and you, he, she, it, one, and they as well as ze, shi, zhim, mer, thon, and co. Quite a few years ago, in the Winter 1982 number of *New Literary History*, I gave an example of a narrative not yet written "a novel in the third person [...] in diary form, using the future tense, and presenting events in a non-chronological order." It still has not been written. I also envisaged a doubly repetitive narrative recounting *n* times (say, fifteen or twenty times) what takes place *n* times. I think that it has met with the same fate. On the other hand, I did, myself, produce countless narratives recounting 0 times what occurs 0 times.

Other dimensions of writing, for instance topographical ones, are considerably less exploited. If John Barth's "Frame-tale" (1968) is a Möbius strip, if Marc Saporta's *Composition No. 1* (1961) or Robert Coover's "Heart Suit" (2005) comprise a set of self-contained pages that can be shuffled like a deck of cards, and if there are numerous pop-up books or movable ones that involve images as well as words, there are not, to my knowledge, that many novels with three-dimensional pages. There are even fewer four-dimensional texts, in which time constitutes the fourth dimension and words, sentences, paragraphs (randomly) appear or disappear.

One area of writing which, when it comes to form, has yielded few experimental products is criticism. On February 8, 2016, as I was getting ready to write this paper, I googled "experimental criticism" and was referred to C. S. Lewis's *An Experiment in Criticism* (1961), a set of posts on cognition, evolution, and literary theory, and a blog entry gesturing toward experimental philosophy and wondering about experiments in criticism. Searches for "experiments in criticism," "experiments in critical form," "formal experiments in criticism," and much more proved equally disappointing in identifying formally innovative and exploratory critical works. Wikipedia did not prove any more helpful. Though it had entries on experimental philosophy, experimental psychology, experimental economics, experimental pop, and many references to experimental writing, it kept mum about experimental criticism. Nevertheless, this kind of critical work does exist. I think that Roland Barthes's *S/Z* (1970) as well as its 1951 forerunner, Léon Bopp's *Commentaire sur Madame Bovary* (1951), Jacques Derrida's *Glas* (1974), Eugène Ionesco's *Nu* (1934), Jean-Michel Raynaud's *Pour un Perec lettré, chiffré* (1985) (which favors the subjunctive), and T. J. Clark's *The Sight of Death: An Experiment in Art Writing* (2006) (thank you Alex Alberro and Nora Alter) all qualify. There is also the conceptual criticism (reminiscent of conceptual art) that is found in innumerable conference submissions and grant proposals or the appropriation criticism that regularly appears in journals and books. I, too, produced a couple of (admittedly timid) experimental pieces of critical writing. I wrote an article, for a 2000 special number of *Style* on narrative, entirely in the form of questions (almost entirely: the editor persuaded me to eliminate the question marks after the title and after my name). Inspired by texts in *Reader's Digest* such as "I Am Joe's Heart" or "I Am Mary's Spleen," I also published an article, in *ST&TCL* (2012), on Michel Houellebecq's *Les Particules élémentaires* (1998) featuring the novel itself as autodiegetic narrator. Still, the fact remains that experimental criticism is waiting to be developed. Perhaps its time has come.

Apart from conceptual criticism and appropriation criticism, there could be (more) hypercriticism (exploiting hypertextual possibilities), microcriticism ("Proust is a yente"), and twitriticism. There could be anagrammatic, paragrammatic, palindromic, or lipogrammatic criticism (as Gérard Genette might say, "Marcel Proust is an exquisitely bright and unnervingly powerful novelist" is a lipogram in d, j, k, and z). There could be unconstructed or deconstructed criticism, providing the reader with a set of phrases, words, or letters to combine meaningfully into a critical construction or reconstruction (as in "rsSaignaedt" or "attribute blue the to likes color Sartre emotions to"). Critics might explicitly resort to cut-up and fold-in techniques, bring into play all the resources of typography, try different kinds of layout, use headnotes instead of footnotes, and critical works might take the shape of an index or a crossword puzzle, mimic the form of riddles, recipes, or jokes, offer multiple possible beginnings, middles, and ends, adopt the imperative or negative mode, alternate different languages (in comparative literature papers), or consist of the bits and pieces, the unpolished phrases, the hesitant developments usually discarded in arriving at a finished product (I believe that quite a few critics resort to this practice. I know I do, though unsystematically).

Now, one may wonder why experimental criticism has not attracted more practitioners. Perhaps this is due to critical circumspection and *esprit de sérieux* or to the weight of institutional constraints or to the power of tradition. But perhaps this also relates to the function of criticism, which is to evoke, account for, situate, describe, interpret, and evaluate (constituent elements of) texts. Perhaps formal experimentation weakens the effectiveness of criticism by obscuring its critical thrust and defeating it. After all, unreliable narrators are certainly welcome in works of fiction but not necessarily in works of history. Similarly, however beautiful or intriguingly shaped a knife may be, it will not quite do as a knife if it does not cut well, and however formally innovative and interesting a critical piece may prove, it will not necessarily be rewarding as a critical piece. But perhaps formal experimentation can enhance the understanding and appreciation of texts by mimicking them or pointing to some of their aspects through the very form it takes. Perhaps it can encourage us to reflect on what the tasks of criticism and the most appropriate formal ways of fulfilling them are. Perhaps it can so frustrate us, disappoint us, or bewilder us that it can make us turn to other, more conventional, critical sources (I know that, after reading a bit of *Glas*, I like to read a bit of *Saint Genet* [1952]). Besides, though no entity can be successful in every capacity (Beethoven is great but not for ballroom dancing) and though criticism may have no apparent affinity with formal experimentation, perhaps some experimental criticism can be formally as well as contentually inventive and thus combine the useful and the pleasant. Perhaps it is just a matter of dosage. Perhaps. The proof will be in the pudding.

28

African Performance and Experimental Traditions
Brian Quinn

We often think of experimental theater as that which pushes the boundaries of conventional performance in pursuit of something fundamentally new. In the American context, an experimental troupe such as the Wooster Group might employ a range of multimedial effects in their stage creations, at times performing in sync with them and at others seeming defiantly disconnected in work that breaks with several theatrical conventions, among them the distinction between live and recorded performance. Experimental theater artists often conceptualize their work as tapping into a source that is timelessly old. The director Richard Schechner famously sought to establish a spectrum of performance that incorporated ancient rites and rituals as well as Western proscenium-style stage plays. In Europe, British director Peter Brook revolutionized the Parisian theatrical scene by looking past the Western canon to create his stage adaptation of the ancient Indian epic the *Mahabharata*. Throughout Brook's career, he has acknowledged his debt to the visionary writings of Antonin Artaud, whose groundbreaking text, "On the Balinese Theatre," was written after attending a performance of Balinese dance at the Paris International Colonial Exposition in 1931, and now constitutes a landmark moment in the Western tradition of experimental theater. This short list of experimental references highlights the broad temporal and geographic variety of inspiration cited by experimental theater artists. It also indicates the emergence of an artistic lineage, a "tradition" that has coalesced around the pursuit of dismantling theatrical traditions.

Myths and representations surrounding the African continent are a frequent focal point of this same experimental tradition. In the case of France, audiences were at times captivated and at others revolted by the use of African subjects in the performance of traditional life at the colonial expositions of the early twentieth century. While these "human zoos" drew the condemnation, in 1931, of France's surrealist writers, the exposition remains a foundational moment in Western experimental theatre by virtue of its role in Artaud's later vision. In the late 1950s, at the twilight of the French colonial project in Africa, the performance worlds of Europe and the US were taken by storm by the theatrical and dance creations of Guinean choreographer Fodéba Keïta. Meanwhile, the troupe of African stage actors called *La Compagnie des Griots* played an integral role in the avant-garde theater of France, particularly in its collaboration with director Roger Blin to stage Jean Genet's explosive work, *The Blacks* (1958).

These examples help to illustrate the undeniable presence of African performers amidst the creative fever pitch of experimental theater's rise. However, in their use of tradition, they also reinforce a certain preconceived notion regarding the relationship between the traditional and the experimental, which sees the experimental as taking its inspiration from notions of the traditional. This relationship is often understood as unidirectional. It would appear illogical to suggest that the traditional may take inspiration from the experimental. We tend to place the two along a chronological line, even in the age when tradition has been so effectively deconstructed as being itself the result of continual reworking and reinvention.

African theater has long constituted the collectively imagined exemplar in the West of traditional performance practice in everyday life. Even in our acknowledgements of ritual as a form of theatrical performance, we tend to conceptualize it as stemming from time immemorial and therefore as unaffected or unaltered by individual acts of innovation or experimentation. A number of important anthropological studies have worked to correct this notion, such as Z. S. Strother's seminal work on Pende sculpture in *Inventing Masks: Agency and History in the Art of the Central Pende* (1998). However, the implications of such work have yet to dawn on certain corners of our worldview and academic disciplines. This disciplinary disjunction makes African theater a fruitful terrain from which to reconsider the interplay of the traditional and the experimental, suggesting that the former can indeed take inspiration from the latter. That is, traditional performance (or the performance of tradition) can reference specifically the tradition of experimentalism (the Western avant-garde) and/or show itself to be fundamentally experimental in its own right.

Take, for example, an international theater festival that is now largely forgotten but that was once a global hotbed for the theatrical avant-garde. In 1954, cultural impresario Claude Planson founded The International Dramatic Arts Festival of the City of Paris, an annual festival that, in 1957, became known simply as The Theater of Nations. This event placed Paris at the center of an emerging notion of what we might today call a world theater. It invited troupes from throughout the globe to the Sarah Bernhardt Theater to represent for Parisian audiences and the theatrical profession at large the performance traditions of a panoply of nations. In 1960, the year of independence for many former African colonies, the festival first invited troupes from the African continent in the spirit of including these traditional forms within an expanding universal understanding of theatrical performance. For festival organizers and commentators, these examples of danced and sung traditional theater stood out as illuminating foils to a European theatrical tradition they saw as doomed to decadence by its long attachment to the written word. A counter model to the European approach was developed and promoted in the form of total theater, that is, a "total" approach to performance in which music, dance and visual storytelling are placed on equal footing, and at times above, any use of scripted text. The traditional works then being imported from Africa fit the parameters of this new category perfectly, using a mixture of ritual, music and dance to present audiences with an event they would have otherwise been more likely to encounter in the pages of a French ethnography than on a Parisian stage.

The list of European and North American participants in the Theater of Nations reads like a *Who's Who* of the experimental movement that soon followed. Successive programs included a production of Bertolt Brecht's *The Caucasian Chalk Circle* (1944), Peter Brook's staging of Shakespeare's *Titus Andronicus* featuring Laurence Olivier and Vivien Leigh, alongside shows by The Living Theatre, and English director Joan Littlewood's groundbreaking production *Oh What a Lovely War!* These were featured alongside performances of Noh, Bunraku, Bharata Natyam and traditional African theater. Of primary concern to the programmers of the Theater of Nations festival was the representational authenticity of the troupes chosen. For this reason, in the case of the African delegates, it befell the directorship of French cultural centers abroad to make a selection on the festival's behalf with the understanding that the centers would send the forms of traditional performance least spoiled by contact with French culture. This of course excluded from festival participation any number of aspiring African playwrights and directors, and instead put the cultural centers, seen as the outposts of French influence, in the role of programmer-ethnographers in their perilous search for authenticity. This need for unspoiled traditionalism came to the surface tellingly when, during the festival's 1960 conference on "Black Theater," Senegalese director Maurice Sonar Senghor (nephew of President Léopold Senghor) suggested that Western theatre professionals assist aspiring African playwrights and theater practitioners. The festival's organizer, Claude Planson, flew into a rage, insisting that African theater should shield its own tradition from the errors of a European theater made impotent by its devotion to narrative storyline and the written word. In this exchange one hears the principles of an experimental theater in Europe determined to "drain abscesses collectively," as Artaud famously put it, of the horrors of two world wars. We also hear the beginnings of a European dichotomization of African theater between the timeless traditional and those who would seek merely to imitate, so to speak, tired, old European stage conventions.

It is no secret that Europe's avant-garde frequently got its start through mimetic contemplation of the East or of the Global

South. Less considered are the ways in which this encounter with the avant-garde inspired or altered forms of traditional performance. The concept of total theater, its intellectual lineage reaching back to Wagner's vision of a total work of art, has fallen out of vogue in European experimental theater. Its heyday and champion came no doubt with the great French director Jean-Louis Barrault, who took over the direction of the Theater of Nations in 1965. However, that same concept has survived and indeed thrived in Africa as the primary form in which to stage pieces of traditional African performance, interweaving song, dance, visual effects (such as masquerade) and storytelling. Authenticity is one of the key principles of a piece of total theater in Africa, much as it was for the French programmer-ethnographers seeking traditional performance pieces to present to an eager avant-gardist European audience. Thus, the presentation and reinvention of traditionalism in the African context finds itself deeply influenced by its encounter with European experimental performance.

A discussion of Africa's place in the world of contemporary experimental theater could easily focus on the prominent playwrights and directors currently working within a hybrid, experimental framework, as influenced by the Western avant-garde as they are by African traditionalism. In the francophone context, Kossi Efoui's poetic piece *Io* comes to mind, as does all of the work of Koffi Kwahulé. European institutions are slowly walking back from Claude Planson's stated position at the Theater of Nations by including in their programming works by emerging theater artists like Dieudonné Niangouna, whose multimedia pieces have now toured throughout Europe. This development has come about largely thanks to the longstanding efforts of institutions like The Francophone Theater Festival in Limoges, which is dedicated to the work of non-European francophone playwrights. In 2017, the illustrious Avignon Theater Festival organized a discussion on African theater, raising, among other questions, the issue of why African theater has produced so few written theatrical works compared to the abundance of stage pieces based on traditional music, dance and folklore. An historical perspective on African theater's long relationship with the avant-garde, and the latter's at times rigid attachment to a timeless notion of traditional performance, may serve as a partial response to such inquiries. However, we may wish to consider this and other questions without relegating traditional, or neo-traditional performance to a category of timelessness that denies this form's ability to be as capable of being inspired as it is of inspiring.

29
Experimental Life
Eleni Sikelianos

The Italian philosopher Giorgio Agamben, whom poets love to quote, writes of what he calls "bare life," the human stripped of its social and political significance and of its specific life form, a kind of remainder or remnant.

The self as less than a shadow of itself.

This, said Lyn Hejinian in a recent talk for the PhiloSOPHIA conference in Denver, can be thrown up against a life being lived in context.

In a human world that seems to display a wild indifference to living

In a culture that seems to care little about cultural production

In a language that has been wielded to betray

On a planet tired of these antics

Because the shape of the future is more anonymous than ever

What is the context?

Where and how do we live?

I mean each of us, but I also mean collectively

The experiment now is very much to figure out how to live

What does this mean for the experiment?

In a living world in which life forms are rapidly disappearing

My concerns now, as a so-called experimental poet, are different than they were

Maybe not from when I was a young proto-poet, when I believed poetry could change the world

When I wanted to tear everything apart and start anew

Not quite knowing that we are connected by memory to the

past, which is the world

But certainly from when I was dedicated to the poetic performance of language above all else

Now it has come to seem that culture-making and art-making are preservationist acts

For salvaging some thinking and feeling among the tatters

I hope this doesn't make making inherently conservative

(Should I be writing to hasten the demise of humans, to save more room and time for the other animals and the plants?)

My understanding of experimental writing for a long time was as a gesture highly concerned with the material

That is certainly like the experiment of living organisms, via evolution

But to test the material, to make it work, living things have to move it through the world

What is moving the material is not entirely the material itself, but is what is alive

Aristotle called this (life) animation

Movement connects one part of the body to another, foot to ankle

As well as one living being to another, fox to mouse

This could be called systems theory but it can also be called context

It could possibly be called content, and at a stretch, turned sideways, landscape

It calls out to another of life's experiments, which is symbiogenesis

The making of new material via collaborative acts rather than competitive ones

One cell sliding into another one

Like a word back into its womb

Or how poets linger on the resonances of word and world in the same chamber

We can call these cells and words communities of interacting entities

Which do not obey the unsmiling reason of the fittest

For a time, it seemed that to be experimental you had to engage in a kind of stern logic

(Gloss: educated or institutionalized logic)

That the irrational, emotional, intuitive, dream life, self-life was for sissies

But just as the self keeps rushing back to language (to paraphrase Hejinian again)

So too does the delirious

As inter/action is a kind of delirium

This seems important in a time when our minds are inextricably entwined in technology

I would say locked in a struggle with " "

But struggle is not the word

Vine in the hive

Does it choke or connect?

There is certainly a weakening of the mind, its intentions and attentions

Its sociability among communities

Of ideas

Of living environments

We are at risk of forgetting how to talk to one another, in sentient context

To live with one another

(It is tempting to go into war statistics here, refugee status, mass extinctions, but also the rise of the thought police

As Dawn Lundy Martin put it recently, "There is no safe space")

What is the purpose of the experiment?

What do we learn from it?

What do we expose?

What life do we make of it?

To challenge not just the material

Which is perhaps analogous, on its own, to bare life

What I am saying

I am understanding just now

Is that to consider only material in the abstract (like capital or language)

Is a way of reducing us to bare life

But to consider material's animation, its movement and interactions

Means to take spiritual, emotional, political, personal and material risks in the poem

And these things (we will call them) together are what make context

(from the Latin: to weave together)

Which is a way to live in the world

"Life did not take over the globe by combat, but by networking," wrote Lynn Margulis and Dorion Sagan together

I sometimes wonder if the technosphere is not mimicking the spiritual(ist)

And this is part of our current challenge—how to create context from the outside for this network

When I say material I do mean syntax (from the Greek: *sun+taxis*, together arrange)

Look how our sun taxis are lined up according to principles and processes

And rearrange

I see syntax as an extension of biology, branching from nature

In it, we can let language wobble fruitfully, like the gene

When I say material I also mean the movement into form (Medieval *formen*, to create, give life to—also, body-shapes)

And the sound of each word rubbing up against the others

The rhythm of each jostling in its context

Rhythm being one of the things that animates the living

First we gave language to the body, comparing it to nests and snakes

Then language began to be evacuated of the body

We lost words for face

But poets know poiesis is to make

As is facere, which is also to face

To make a face

A face (a form) (shared root)

To face up to it

To self-make

Face to face

As in a mirror
To eye
To see
Tongue
Tooth
Neck
Throat
Shoulder
Arm
Elbow
Hand
Finger
Thigh
Knee
Ankle
Foot
Toe
Nail
Claw
Wing
Feather
Breast
Udder
Navel
Heart
Liver

To put your antique forehead up against them all
And look
Un-inveigling
To see that face is not wiped clean of its features

30

Norms and Experimental Knowing
Alan Singer

Is literature ever *not* experimental?

If one could answer in the affirmative, one would have to consent to the proposition that literary norms are at odds with the nature of norm-making itself. I do not hesitate to add that making is the experiential link to aesthetic objects and, more to the point, a link to understanding norms as coherent with making art. Normativity is often misguidedly cast as the dogmatic antagonist to free spirited imagination. But, for the true experimentalist, I think it is hard to imagine how one is possible without the other. Partisans of pure imagination presumptuously and deprecatingly take norms to be already made. As we know, this is an assumption long and deftly debunked by Duchamp's deployment of the ready-mades. So, by indulging an invidious comparison of normativity and originality, we obscure the origin of norms.

If we can become more nuanced in our thinking about norms, we realize that things turn normative out of an exigency of unintelligibility, out of a circumstance that throws up obstacles to one's self-understanding, one's knowing what to think and what to do next. I would say that the normative "turn" turns out very much like the turn in a sonnet or the reversal of fate in a dramatic plot. One wants to know why one can't make sense of the conundrum of the next moment. This, for me, is the ineluctable condition of fiction-making and of living a responsible life: keeping faith with the contingency of one's otherwise over-confident self-knowledge. One must avoid the trap of too self-pre-emptively knowing oneself. This avoidance is the vocation of the experimentalist.

So, I start with the notion that norms do not inexorably make a dogma of knowledge. They are its condition of possibility as well. I could say even more strongly that norms betoken possibility. This is a counter-intuitive claim only if we forget that norms come from some place that is non-normative. We can take norms to be obstacles to new knowledge only when normative values are divorced from the practice of value-making as an ongoing activity. As Marshall McLuhan famously observed, one can't make a grammatical mistake in a preliterate society. One needs norms in order to grasp imaginatively, the conditions that they do not yet govern. McLuhan echoes Nietzsche's uncompromising empirical intuition that when we speak of moral norms we are recognizing the actions of an exceptional individual. The exceptional individual breaks with herd mentality. In that gesture, she makes normativity count for herself and, implicitly, for those whose identity is discoverable by exigent activity rather than any inherited, and all too well assimilated, tradition.

So, let us resist the temptation to think of experimental art as radically different from experimental behavior. We behave according to conventional mandates to be sure. But nothing is mandated without the caveat that expected conformity to the mandate devolves unexpectedly to improvisational behavior. Even non-conformity has a form. This is to admit that norms involve us in formative activity: an invitation to the unintended consequence. For this reason, let us indulge the hypothesis that experimentalism is neither culture specific nor inexorably bounded by historical convention. Let us accordingly dispense with the folly of privileging the *avant-garde* as a necessary condition for experimentalism. Jean-François Lyotard has lamented the *avant-garde's* betrayal of its responsibility to knowledge almost as soon as the term came into currency at the end of the nineteenth century. I approve of Lyotard's will to conflate knowledge with research activity, whereby we do not presuppose the terms according to which we would promise advancement. Lyotard dabbles, so to speak, in the history of the *avant-garde* of painting. For him a figure like Cézanne is exemplary. Cézanne does not paint. He asks the question, "What is painting?" Cézanne is a quintessential experimentalist because his stance, when he is making forms, is rigorously interrogative.

The question for Cézanne, as it should be for all of us if we are animated by the experimental spirit, is not what is a successful experiment, but what can experimentation tell us about itself/ ourselves in the act of exploiting our experimental acumen? The artist's experimental gambit is never merely about surprise. Counter-intuitively, surprise only tells us what we already know too well. The signature shock of vaunted *avant-garde* literature is little more than recognition that one's fragile expectations have been revealed in all of their fragility. Expectations are the residue of experience. Better to know what we do not yet know, except as the exigency of our existing in relation to an unpredictable world of unfolding events.

I am eschewing the notion then that there is such a thing as an "experimental principle" governing the experimenter. The operative "principle," is the circumstantiality of the question: what does it mean? The "it" is everything. For "it" only ever means anything in a specific time, a specific place, in the grip of a specific desire to inhabit time and place as one's own world. Possessiveness, however, is not the point. Experimentalism belongs to experience. It does not capture experience. One's own world, in the purview I take up here, is the world of possibility, with the caveat that that possibility cannot be conflated with pure indeterminacy, which would inevitably moot the formalistic/ formative aspect of the enterprise. That is the source of its vitality and its only resemblance to life that literature can meaningfully keep faith with. Absent the possibility of formal articulation, the literary experimenter is doomed to become an ever more self-mystifying metaphysician.

Henry Green might be a name to conjure with in my effort to break experimentalism out of the institutional laboratories of academic debate over the "nature" of experimental literature. The protocols of the laboratory, the women and men in white coats who would be testing for evidence of an *avant-garde's* cutting edge, who would be culturing the act of surprise, and probing for the reflexive defiance of rationality would be, for all their portending of unprecedented novelty, skewed from the commonplaces of actual imaginative invention. I mention Green because he is one of

those writers whose "experimentalism' is perennially redis-
covered, as if he were still alive and writing on into an
unimaginable future. The decision of New York Review Books to
republish Green's oeuvre this year, attended by reviews that evince
amazement at how Green's language reawakens the reader to his
or her capacity for linguistic rapport with the world in the first
place, is testimonial to the fact that experimentalism—Green's
emphatically—is intrinsic to the *ongoingness* of life. It is not a stop
in time. It is not a break with normativity. It is how normativity
sustains engagement with the contingency, the mutability, of our
human circumstance. I would agree that the effect of reading
Green, in such animating novels as *Caught* (1943), *Back* (1946),
and *Party Going* (1939) especially, is the impression that one is in
fluent possession of a language that is not entirely one's own. In
publishing, Green keeps coming back. But he does not come back
as the reliable, recognizably old experimentalist Henry Green. It is
as if he was always there, ever in the capacity of the innovator, but
never "caught," so to say, in the recognizable gesture of
experimentalism.

Consequently, it is difficult to monumentalize Green's
novels as experiments, in the manner we are accustomed to do
when we valorize experimentation as a trait of high literariness.
Think Joyce, Eliot, Pound etc. Green's "eternal return," acutely
attunes readers to the fact that every word choice on the part of the
author is a counterpart to a reader's willingness to defer
knowledge, as well as to claim it. The power of such deference
inheres in our faith that there is more knowledge to come. Our
persisting, and in that way ordinary, fascination with Green's
novels, has in great part to do with the fact that they situate us in
stunningly ordinary worlds of human activity: factories, train
stations, quasi-documentary scenarios of the London blitz, country
houses-mostly downstairs affairs. Green's experimentalism has
little to do with conspicuous literary maneuvers: eliminating a
letter of the alphabet, spatially disorienting typographical layouts,
labyrinthine streams of consciousness, chance operations,
appropriating allegorical structures from antiquity or from the
technologies of emerging culture. But my intent here is not to make
invidious comparisons with writers who are famous for trading in

these familiar hallmarks of experimentalism. I am certainly not setting Green up as the "real experimentalist."

I am more interested in Green's return as an epitome of how normative predictability is inextricable from knowing the unpredictable. Consider a passage from Green's novel *Caught,* quoted in Allen Hollinghurst's review of the new edition of Green's novels and purveyed as proof of Green's experimentalism: "The relief he experienced when their bodies met was like the crack on a snow silent day, of a branch that breaks to fall under a weight of snow, as his hands went like two owls in daylight over the hills, moors and wooded valleys, over the fat white winter of her body."

Hollinghurst takes the telltale of Green's originality, his "*sui generis*" experimentalism, to be "unexpected metaphor." I would rather say, since I have already dismissed "mere surprise," as a valid touchstone of experimentalism, that it is Green's dramatization of the act of knowing, unimpeded by knowledge as a burdensome content of efficient human agency, that is the revelatory aspect of his prose in this case. I would say that in the quoted passage the *fatness of winter* is what arises as a new horizon of intelligibility that is not self-pre-empting conceptual punctuation. It incentivizes intelligibility as an ability. It does not confirm intelligence.

My choice to be illustrative with the practices of Henry Green is in no way meant to be a blanket denigration of the widely recognized devices of experimental writing. I only wish to shift emphasis away from the counter-intuitively instrumental notion that experimentalism is exclusively device-activated. I would rather articulate a cautionary about the canned knowledge that the utility of any such experimental devices is unconsciously indebted to, if our practice of experimentation does not bring that fact to consciousness, and thereby render it an act of knowing in its own right. After all, this indebtedness underscores my sense that normativity and experimentation are symbiotic with respect to the vitality of knowing anything that matters.

Is it any surprise that when Green submitted himself to the experiment of orchestrating a cagily self-explanatory BBC radio talk ("A Novelist to His Reader," 1950), his one reluctant admonition was that the writer himself must resist the temptation to narrate. For Green the indulgence of narration was most egregiously the inducement to become a "know all." The know all knows what he thinks in a vacuum of activity. But Green is neither an irrationalist nor a willful know-nothing. Green cultivated a passionate interest in human unknowability, but not as an unknowing mystification of human being. I would say that unknowability for Green is, like normativity to imagination, an intimation that there is something more to be done than what one already knew to be the case. And this requires active thinking. Just consider how dialogue without narration is the portent of knowledge, more than the expression of it. Where dialogue is the case, riposte is always in the air. Dialogue, often without attribution, always on a trajectory into the future, was one of Green's signal formal/form-making gambits. Green's métier recalls one to the excitement of a multi-dimensional human circumstance.

For me circumstantiality is the *sine qua non* of experimentation. To conjure a circumstance and then to respect its porous temporal boundaries, to intensify human responsiveness to the world, is to keep faith with possibility. Otherwise, as even Aristotle intuited by privileging action above character in *Poetics*, human circumstance is flattened. It is reduced to the one dimensionality of the merely representable.

31

Experimentalism, Then and Now
Cole Swensen

As Mallarmé said in 1896, there is a crisis in poetry. This isn't always the case; there are eras that go by without them, eras of relative aesthetic harmony and fluidity, but this is not one of them, which is a good thing, as only poetry in crisis is interesting. Poetry not in crisis is poetry complacent, settled, and therefore not doing what poetry, socially and culturally, needs to do, which is to be agitated, and then to agitate, in turn.

By a "crisis in poetry," I don't mean to say that something is happening *to* poetry, but that poets themselves are effecting a distinct change in the medium, which tends to put the medium at risk. That said, it's also helpful to remember that the word crisis derives from the Greek *krinein* "to decide" and its noun form *krisis* or "decision," which makes available a less dramatic while more measured and more focused interpretation of the term.

It's poetry's potential for crisis that allows it to function as a "minor" in relation to the "major" of prose in the way that Deleuze and Guattari intended in their development of the concept of a minor language. Their work looked at the ways in which the literature of a minority community written, not in a "minor" language, but in the language of the majority community works to destabilize the major literature because the very existence of the minor literature constitutes a constant disruption—a constant agitation—of the dominant one. The minor is always, to some degree, in their terminology, deterritorialized, a state that combines traits of the deracinated and the indeterminate, thus, on the one hand, the unprotected and the estranged, and on the other, the liberated and the unbounded.

Though Deleuze and Guattari were talking about minor and major bodies of literature in very specific linguistic and cultural contexts, there's a way in which all poetry acts as a minor literature to all prose, regardless of the language, and it's poetry's capacity to remain indefinitely in a state of crisis, of disequilibrium, that allows it to compromise, constantly and subtly, the prosaic principles of clarity and stability. To the prosaic dream of a 1:1 relationship of word to meaning, poetry proposes any other ratio—and therefore has many more compositional options than prose. And yet, despite that increased range and flexibility, poetry never becomes the dominant. This is in part because the vast majority of any language's user value, above all, its clarity and stability, and are therefore not open to its destabilizations, no matter how aesthetically intriguing they might be. But above all, poetry never becomes major because only by remaining the minor to prose can it continue its disruptive relationship to it, a relationship that allows it to act as a force that constantly causes prosaic language to keep refining, redefining, and reinventing itself, thereby avoiding a debilitating stasis. Poetry speaks the same language as prose, but speaks it differently and, as such, continually infects prose with difference, keeping it changing. And as prose changes, poetry also changes—though, often it is the changes in poetry that instigate those in prose. A victorious circle, one might say.

To a certain extent, there's a relationship between linguistic instability and experimentalism—and here, by linguistic instability, I mean everything that compromises that 1:1 ratio, all the traditional markers of the poetic, which are, by and large, all the aspects of a language other than the semantic, such as its sound qualities and sound relationships as well as ambiguity, parataxis, and figurative language, among others. In general, the more exaggerated those markers are, the more a work is experienced as experimental.

The poetic in this sense was the project of a crisis in American poetry that dominated the late 1970s through the 1990s. Centered in a crisis of meaning, it explored the limits of sense and the non-semantic potentials of language, resulting in a new appreciation of the wide range of linguistic elements beyond the semantic. That crisis helped poetics as a field identify and research those elements, understanding their inner workings and developing their potentials, making non-semantic linguistic elements more readily available as artistic materials, getting readers more sensitized and open to them, and generally broadening the definition of meaning by foregrounding language's materiality.

Though many of these experiments focused on materiality, they put oddly little emphasis on the materiality of sound. Instead, these works more often explored modes of disjunction that threw a tremendous weight onto associative fields. The connotative networks surrounding every word get emphasized when chains of words and phrases resist an accumulative meaning—not able to go forward, we go outward, and in ever-widening circles that bring increasingly distant contingencies into the composite experience. As a body, the products of those experiments emphasized the "field" in myriad ways, from networked rather than linear meaning, as described above, to a reconsideration of the page as a visual field.

The tremendous gains occasioned by that crisis and its attendant experiments made it possible for poets working in the past twenty years to return to semantic meaning with an enriched set of possibilities. This has emerged, in the past fifteen to twenty years, in a reconsideration of statement, a reconsideration of the relationship of language to fact, in which non-semantic aspects of language are consciously used to pressure the semantic in various ways.

Fact is always twofold: there is its existence as event, and there is its preservation in language, with the second determining, which is to say, irremediably altering the first. A fact's existence as a time-based event necessarily and instantaneously vanishes, and the statement remains—with no one's having any way of ascertaining or proving its veracity. And thus, the statement becomes the "truth," overriding that of the event. This is rarely questioned. One *tells* the truth—one doesn't see the truth or hear the truth or feel the truth. Of course one does, initially, see and hear and feel it, but only if one happens to be present, and even in that case, once the moment has passed, language takes over, and telling becomes the only body that truth can adopt. And it is an adoption—

i.e., there is a disruption in the line of descent. That doesn't necessarily mean that the telling is unfaithful, but a difference has inevitably and irremediably been inscribed.

The current crisis in poetry is focused right there, in that disruption in the line. It queries, first, the transformation of event into language—who carries out this transformation? And from what perspective and in what context? It also explores the ways that making use of language's non-semantic elements as well as of its semantic ones, elements that interrupt sense as normally understood, can offer a more accurate presentation of event. In other words, it's precisely the break-downs in language that can represent aspects of experience that cannot be represented in language.

The elements that can offer that representation are just those elements that distinguish language-as-art-material from language-as-information-constructor. Focusing on that distinction, this crisis is manifest in movements as diverse as documentary poetry and spoken word, many of which have distinct social, political, and cultural goals. Some poets are using these elements to respond to a parallel crisis of social justice in the US; others are engaging with discoveries and developments in the sciences and technology and others with personal issues, including the body, identity, and family, and still others with the climate crisis in a movement known as ecopoetics. Despite their wide range of concerns and styles, they all participate in an attempt to interfere with the seemingly seamless production of information in order to highlight the problematics of that apparent seamlessness.

In this way, the current crisis is particularly engaged with its "minorist" potential. It directly addresses the informational language that is usually the sole purview of prose, infusing it with various multiplicities. Such work not only questions the nature of information but also the nature of art by putting pressure on the distinction and exploring the point at which the one tips over into the other. Much of this work seeks ultimately to establish a different relationship between language as an art material and language as information, one in which the art aspects play a greater role in a broad range of discourses, broadening them in turn.

The same non-semantic elements operate in many kinds of

writing that are not considered poetry as such—in fact, in all well-written prose, but also in a variety of highly public forms that range from advertising to op-eds to political speeches—but only in poetry do they act overtly rather than covertly, which subtly points to the more insidious uses in other spheres.

Many contemporary writers working in documentary and research-based modes have an interest in undermining "knowledge" as a set category, with the hope of enlarging its definition. These works implicitly ask what counts as knowledge and how that accounting is established; how knowledge differs from experience, and where and when it is possible or appropriate to make that distinction; what the relationship is between knowledge and a variety of other phenomena, such as memory, recording, and other forms of accountability. The question of *who* comes up again and again—who answers all of these questions?—and clearly, the only correct answer is *everyone*. Addressing the constitution of information as an initial step in the constitution of knowledge and achieving a broader participation in both requires a broader language—and speakers of that language who make conscious and ethical use of all of its resources, not just the semantic ones.

32

I Joined the Avant-Garde to Save the World and All I Got
    Was This Goofy Red Hat
Steve Tomasula

WTF. For real? I'm not being facetious because I'd really like to know: Was the election of The Donald the crowning achievement of the avant-garde? Some Krazy Kartoon where Daffy Duck, Betty Boop, Mr. Natural and a host of others are pursuing a Bozo-haired Mr. Monopoly, and just before they really get the LOSER, Boris and Natasha draw a trap door that drops him into the Oval Office.

This was not your grandma's avant-garde even if her name wasn't Gertrude. Then again, maybe it was. For there were many avant-gardes, and among them we have to count Italian Futurism whose Manifesto includes gems like Article 9: "We will glorify war—the world's only hygiene—… and scorn for woman."

It's beyond the limits of this *cri de cœur* to describe the various forms that the avant-garde took as it changed across time and locals, but most relevant here are two strains of what has been called the last avant-garde, Postmodernism. One can be called Fredric Jameson's 31-Flavors version: Postmodernism as patina, weightless, meaningless simulation and play in a climate of "boundless capitalism" where the market determines what is good, or worth attention.

The other version, let's call it "The Sugar Coated Pill" version, more associated with François Lyotard who "thought of Postmodernism as the triumph of pragmatism, and of efficiency and performativity against the old 'Grand Narratives,'" as Simon During puts it, "notably the narratives of social progress, be they religious eschatology or knowledge's scientification." In this strain, the Emperor of Jameson's Late Capitalism got where he was by wearing new clothes, and Postmodernism was just the boy to see through them: to call out received or "natural" Narratives as constructed, the product of viewpoint and history, and more often than not hegemony.

I want to say, it seemed as though those in the avant-garde, including most of the authors in this anthology, were working toward something.

Then Came the TRAGEDY of 9/11 or The Defeat of the Difficult Poems

Near the end of *The Two Towers*, one of the Hobbits mouths Rambo, John Wayne, Bruce Willis clichés about common folk going to war to fight evil and the audience I was in, during the run up to the Invasion of Iraq, began chanting, "USA! USA!"

A fixed viewpoint is needed for any citizen to see themselves as the hero in their own story. And this is true whether those citizens are Hobbits, ISIS martyrs, Hitler's brown-shirted youth smashing windows for the good of the Fatherland, or red-hatted middle-aged men chanting "Lock Her Up" at stadium rallies. Conversely, from the perspective of the avant-garde, a fixed viewpoint is often the problem: a kind of certainty, or naturalness, that enables patriarchy, dictatorships, homophobia, market goodness, and the bourgeois art of state and church.

After 9/11, though, the avant-garde in general and Postmodernism in particular found itself swimming against a cultural current so strong, that Brian McHale found the collapse of the Twin Towers to be a useful symbol for its end: "a fundamental cultural shift such as we may see only once, perhaps twice, every century or so," as culture critic Julia Keller called it in her essay "After the Attack, Postmodernism Loses Its Grip." Others more directly called for a "more intense rejection" of "ethically perverse" postcolonial theory and postmodern "challenges" to "the notion of objective truth." Or as George Bush put it: "You are either with us or with the terrorists."

Then Came the TRAGEDY of 11/9 or The World Turned Upside Down

The "embrace of chaos...the crisis of representation, fragmentation, alienation...indeterminacy, rupture of certainty—material and symbolic"—these characteristics could easily be used to describe The Donald's campaign and following administration except they were written by critic Marjorie Perloff to describe Postmodernism.

Which is to say, Postmodernism didn't go away; its methods were adopted by the right, albeit with completely different goals, mainly to entrench rather than open power structures. If you say BLM, they turn it into WLM; if you characterize them as Alt-Right; they call you the Alt-Left. One might call it Applied Postmodernism, of the Neo-liberal, 31-Flavors variety: an emergent effort to cast reality as constructed, along with a number of issues with pivotal importance: everydayness, history, gender, especially as they are represented. By unmasking language as ambiguous, racism can be recast as "heritage" and "gay marriage" can be constructed as the oxymoron that it "is"; by exposing scientific consensus as "point of view," global warming can be seen as a conspiracy to keep coal miners at the bottom of a hierarchy of "elites"....

The ground for this shift had been well prepared by the developments within Postmodernism itself, perhaps most powerfully by the leveling of the high-low divides, amplified by the democratization of the tools of communication. We're all poets now! And videographers! And constitutional experts!—mainly because we all have the means to publish our opinions to a worldwide audience. The cultural forces that allowed literature to become just another flavor of cultural expression, that treats beer commercials with the same critical seriousness as Shakespeare—the sort of pluralism that is inherent in the 31-Flavors version of Postmodernism—contains within it a politics of its own: the marginalization of expertise of all kinds. Should anyone be surprised, then, when the erosion of high-low boundaries comes to politics?—and enough people see nothing wrong in making a game-show host president?

The shock of the new brought to us by The Donald's election was the blitzkrieg of social technologies that leveraged the right-wing's use of rhetorical tools associated with the avant-garde; and it came as a shock because we'd been told so often that these technologies were inherently benign. Facebook was going to bring together families, not neo-Nazis. Twitter would aid pro-democracy movements, not erode the democracy we had in America. Social media was going to make Americans more, not less, informed, as happened when their algorithms helped create echo chambers where rumors and lies could be circulated millions of times by The Donald's supporters, inner circle, and himself, until they became "real."

As though mirroring Krzysztof Ziarek's description of fascist regimes of the past, this home-grown version was going to make America great again by offering "in place of a historical experience a perverse *Gesamtkunstwerk*," the nation state as a "living artwork," and it would do so not through old school reason or the pursuit of truth but by riding the tide of "engagement" (a.k.a. clicks & churn) that was becoming the lingua franca of politics. Big data analysis might reveal that teenagers find prom more meaningful than tax reform, so the algorithms FB uses will channel news of prom to them to keep them engaged; for the bigots who supported The Donald, hate speech is more "engaging and meaningful" than balanced reporting, and contributed to a postmodern world where reality is constructed, and the global became local, lived experience, where citizens consume news that wasn't produced by journalists, or even Russian hackers but by bots programmed to create fake news stories out of trending topics, i.e. "news" that comes out of a place that is no place, has no geography or history, and is "shared" without human intervention: perfect, floating postmodern signifiers.

What's a writer to do? I looked to other places where jouissance and other tools of a theoretically savvy, avant-garde had had to find a way, but only found funhouse mirrors. In places like China, the official fake news was still having its pants pulled down by conceptual artists while back in America it was being written by men in red hats, or teenagers in the Ukraine pretending they were men in red hats pretending they were wearing press badges while the left was pushed deeper and deeper into the conservative aesthetics of social realism: Truth, Beauty, and the American Way.

I tried to think what this could mean for art, and literature, and found myself writing the same words as a Chilean author: That is, in America things were not going well. For me, things had been going well, but not for my country. I am not a fanatical nationalist, and it took very real damage to democracy, and to the ideals that its institutions make possible, to make me realize that the authors I most wanted to be like sincerely did believe in them. America, my America. What on earth has come over you? I would sometimes ask, leaning out my open window and looking at the Tea Party flag hanging from the Leave-It-To-Beaver house across the street. What have they done to you? Have my countrymen gone mad? Who is to blame? And sometimes, walking down an aisle in my university bookstore, with more football jerseys than books, and more books about accounting than literature, and what few books there were shelved under Literature being mostly stories about wizards saving the world, I would ask: How long do you think you can go on like this, America? Are you going to change beyond recognition? Become a monster?

I picked up my remote control. Let god's will be done, I said (by which I meant the market). I'm going to watch TV. Respecting the tradition, I started with *Amos and Andy*, then moved on to *Mr. Ed, Bewitched, Gilligan's Island* (wonderful), *Date My Mom*, and then planes flew into the Twin Towers, and "WMD" came into our vocabulary as General Colin Powell presented pictures of sewer pipes and holes in the ground as evidence for atomic weapons that inspectors who had actually been there said were sewer pipes and holes in the ground, and 600,000 Iraqi civilians went up in flames.

And on TV before every football and baseball game, the announcers salivated with thanks to the military for giving us our freedom (though people in places like Canada or France didn't seem to need endless wars to be free), and the war, which never even ended, became known as a great victory for democracy, instead of a pointless tragedy that needlessly ruined the lives of millions (Mission Accomplished!), and didn't even do away with the relativism of postmodernism, only translated it into Applied Postmodernism: methods to fuzz the boundary between reality and narrative, not as a way to challenge totalizing narratives such as the White Man's burden, but to reinforce power structures, the way cigarette companies fought the link between tobacco and cancer, and oil companies fought the link between burning carbon and heating the earth, not by saying things like black lungs, or submerged towns weren't real, but that the stories of their cause were fictitious, and in horror we watched as words like "truthiness" invented by a comic to parody Republican-speak were trumped by even more Orwellian phrases like "alternative facts." And losing emails became equated with high treason while driving companies into bankruptcy, stiffing workers, discriminating against tenants, conning students, committing fraud, dodging the draft and taxes was equated with being smart, and the Internet empowered my eighty-year-old racist uncle Eddie who helped make what had been known as fact-checking irrelevant, and turned spending money and owning assault rifles into forms of free speech while being the most qualified candidate to ever run for office became a liability, and ignorance, "pussy grabbing," and pushing the doomsday clock closer to nuclear war became assets. Then came the election that placed this monster at our head: the ugliest of Ugly Americans. And alternative facts became official policy, and mass shootings like the one that murdered 26 grade-school kids in Newtown were declared to have been faked and Hillary Clinton's running of a child prostitution ring out of a pizza parlor became a well known "fact," and a man showed up with a rifle, and shot into a closet where he believed her pimps were hiding, and after he was arrested, and it was pointed out that the closet was only a closet, replied, "The Intel was not 100%" on this…." I got up and looked out the window: Peace and quiet. The sky was blue, a deep, clean blue, with a few scattered clouds. I saw a helicopter in the distance. People get the rulers they deserve, I recalled one of our Founding Fathers saying, and we certainly deserved this one—we with our zombies and idiocracy obsession with celebrities, and likes and clicks—and I recalled David Ciccoricco's quote of Malcolm Bradbury from back in the day when everyone was first trying to figure out this thing called Postmodernism: if it "'designates a stylistic, cultural and intellectual epoch that we also call Postwar, then I think it is over. If it designates, as critics like Fredric Jameson argue, the cultural life of late capitalism, its triumph and then its crisis may be just beginning.'"

Leaving the window open, I knelt and prayed, for America, for all Americans, especially those in the avant-garde, the living and the dead.

33

Epic Experiment: Praetexa & Performance
Anne Waldman

in my praetorium in my pragmatic space in my night-alliance-
weaponry-space

all the soldiers bedding down in my dictation in my dictum

I not with them   I apart

& they with armor, and fine of it. all manner of spears, knives,
lance, & drum

swords to swoon by, but I make it clean to do it not wanting this
ever effort spared

& with the praetexta, some with purple border bound as an
assemblage
     that is a weaponeer's eruption system

a kind of mad male delight

come give me my stylet, pen for the blind

a phalanx of twice-handled shield, gone this way and that a
steady show

I would rank now and write Pindaric

close rank now & write a public ode

separate out from him who is pleomorphic

who shifts the atmosphere makes it dawn-deadly the fellows up
now readying
    as they my brothers & are hurting for fight

you of action materialized of archaic consilium & fiscus. you
toads of brutal war

maybe he had me saying: *made crazy by many-tours sooty war*

sooty sooty war, coming out of the dead articulum

to write my cut-throat ode again

    "Ode" from *The Iovis Trilogy: Colors in The Mechanism of
Concealment,* Book III

    Is war an experiment? How is one experimental in poetry
that attempts to document, in addition to throbs and throes of
existence, perpetual conflict, bloody, sooty and ugly crimes
against humanity? Or is there some gnosis in the pleasures of war?

    Ezra Pound's "Sestina Altaforte" comes to mind with its
glee in "the sunrise blood-crimson." Insanity each day in a political
dystopia creates rage. Poets seek imagination's release. Is there
liberation through poetry that bends form and intention? Beyond
the therapeutic? What activates our language motor, our desire to
construct an activist "machine"? My lines above purport to be
experimental. I don the "preatexta" (ceremonial priestly robe) and
interact with melodic drones. Because U.S. of A. is reminiscent at
times of the clumsy, old, bellicose Roman empire I invoked
ceremonial Latin. The word from which "ode" derives is the Attic
"aeidein," to sing. And is patterned after the dance-like structure
of Greek dramatic chorus, with its strophe, anti-strophe, and
epode. This structure in mind influenced the three "books" of the

Iovis poem.

A question: how are poets contemporary with their time? How might they be both postmodern existentialist and ancient seer, and avant-morte as well? How do they inhabit rhythms across time? Gertrude Stein invoked the "continuous present," Pound observed that in the *mind of the poet all times are contemporaneous*. Tracking monsters, nightmares, holocausts, Anna Akmatova, Paul Celan, Raul Zurita among many others come to mind. One summons, invents within language a new ethos of intent, of syntax-in-struggle, and in the case of Celan powerful hybrids: *shardstrewn, wordlight, tearstain*. He spoke of a poem being like a message in a bottle toward "an addressable reality." Poets deconstruct, reconstitute, then re-shatter shards of history into our time, the unhinged late Capitalocene. A poem is allowed to chronicle the history of its own making. The mind of the poet may also be the subject of the poem.

Not made facilely and to not let the owning of other's suffering or even one's own be a begging for sympathy of the poem. To transcend this emotional crux one goes to open form, composition by field, indeterminancy, documentary-poetics, meta-text, hybrid form, dream, obliteration of personal "I." And there are Oulipo strategies of constraint and play such as Georges Perec's "story-making machine" or the experiment of univocalism, a poem using only one vowel letter. I wanted "o" as a searing *cri de coeur*. One may be inspired by another work of art as in ekphrastic practice. Erasure, invisibility. And there is the epic form that is also a performance, a meander. That may cover a species, a life, a time that moves in many directions simultaneously.

Imagine it falls to you (you write out of necessity)—you the solo poet—or the collective "you." And your voice/language/ego is anointed/appointed to tell of your tribe your "gender" your time on earth. Grandiose schemes. I took this as my particular lot, or burden or good fortune when I began my epic project because I needed a female to take on male energy. I was projecting a metaphorical village, a city in conflict with that other one down the road, an earthly neighborhood, story of a war between tribes, families, countries over water rights, hunting rights, religious rites, oil, the Jerusalemic archeological tunnel—the tooth and claw level of *agôn*—contest, struggle—literal or psychic. You might suffer "treedome" as Myrrah does, abused by her father, as recounted in Ovid, who is transformed to weep bitter tears. Same psychic situations exist now but can we not be "translated" as Shakespeare's Bottom is, out of our new millennium traumatic nightmare? You might dance and wear a mask, evolve a "persona." This is instinctual, akin to proprioception: "eyes in all the heads to be looked out of" (Charles Olson). Here where human violence is no less extreme than Beowulf, than Gilgamesh, than Homer, than Dante. And its windows (the windows of that violence) are still also on the stars. One works out of a mythopoetics but worries it, tampers with it, creates meta-text of text outside another text that can time-travel. I took a vow to poetry *as long as we humans we are still killing each other.*

Not the content but the way new form accommodates shift of frequencies. How one jolts from the edge, as in my *Manatee/ Humanity*, which is a longer poem of call and response, environmental urgency, research of animal origins, visits to the museum of skeletons in Paris, and with a particular litany-like modal structure. The poem moves from montage, chance operation, to documentary poetics, to Buddhist ritual where one might create the life stream of the endangered manatee. Yet knowing its origin, as *maniti*, Haitian word for breast, "breast like women's that suckled their young"/Carib manattoui/*Mantouf*/ maybe Mandingo origin/Latinized as *manatus*/infrasound pro- duced in larynx/Ojibwa: *manitoo*/"turned with its hands" is generative. And the science: "the manatee has more grey matter in the brain than man/the manatee is archivally deeper than man/the manatee may be maimed by man, man oh aid the manatee, come to the manatee heart." The litany invokes "tidalectics" (Kamau Braithewaite) through the rhythms of the swimming "mother manatee with her just one offspring." And conjures the manatee as Sirenian. I constantly think about entering public space with multiple voices. And include both the *arche*, the sense of first things, as mind, as larynx, out of things that exist, and the *techne,* the craft, what's operative, *episteme.* Make it *work.*

Years ago I was a poet-emissary to India, representing Allen Ginsberg's Committee On Poetry which was working on a project to bring a number of Indian poets to the U.S. C.O.P would help sponsor and schedule readings and events at Columbia University, the University of California, Berkeley and Naropa University in Boulder. I was the only woman, and American, invited to a festival organized at the Bharat Bhavan arts center in Bhopal. This would be a way to become familiar with a range of writers and performers from India. The Bharat Bhavan was built in 1982 shortly before the industrial disaster at the Union Carbide Plant, a gas leak that killed at least 8,000 people and harmed thousands more. There was finally a settlement in 2010 of a sum under five million dollars, a paltry amount for the massive death and injurious harm. I followed the case for a number of years. Arundhati Roy was outspoken, outraged, lucid. During the visit to Bhopal one observed death-ash on the land, the people, their psyches, and circumambulated the ghostly shanty towns around the Union Carbide plant murmuring Buddhist and Hindu mantras. Like visiting a hell realm. Poet: speak to hell. Bodies and desiccated remnants were still coming to light. The center had a gallery filled with photographs depicting unfathomable suffering. One felt enormous sorrow and outrage at the unconscionable actions and negligence of the parent company, its CEOs, the cynicism of building a compromised site in a desperately poor neighborhood. The calculated response and resistance to accountability was brutal.

What could one do or say but protest, write letters, send money? And I wondered during and after this trip how poetry might gasp the magnitude of restless variegated catastrophe, involving cosmologies, cultures you barely knew; what form, what way of telling? My epic might include Bhopal and would also include Rocky Flats, the site in Colorado where plutonium was put in "pits" for nuclear warheads. Rocky Flats sat astride Boulder and the campuses of the University of Colorado and of Naropa

University and its Jack Kerouac School of Disembodied Poetics. Many citizens, poets, students, activists protested, were arrested, and helped shut the plant down. Allen Ginsberg read his "Plutonian Ode," I chanted "mega mega mega mega death-bomb— enlighten!" Plutonium still resides in the soil.

The Hindu equivalent of hell is Naraka, and it is located in the south of the universe and beneath the earth. Naraka is a pit of darkness not far from where the dead ancestors live. And the Muslim hell, according to the Quran, is called Jahannan and the breadth of each wall in hell is a journey of forty years. It's interesting that within the epic practice in the Pitjantjatjara tradition of Australia's aboriginals, which could be the oldest poetic practice in the world, it may take forty years to become a songman. It is an epic sung continuously over a cycle of twenty years which involves oral travel instructions on a circular migration pattern. The epic will explore where the witchetty grubs live, the sleeping lizards lie, how to survive through a knowledge of local botany. Dreamtime is a poet's dimension, a compendium of knowledge and walking, singing, memorization, and spontaneity as well.

The other participants in the festival at Bharat Bhavan were poets writing in English, Marathi, Hindi, Bengali, Assamese. The poems were classical, some more modernist, but restrained, with the exception of the Vedic singers who performed in Sanskrit, and the Bauls of Bengal who performed a beautiful mix of ancient and contemporary frenzy. I had heard field recordings in the early 1970s, always curious about these ecstatic street-poets. Baul is related to the Sanskrit word "Vatula," which means madcap. A Baul is one possessed, with uncut coiled hair, a necklace of tulsi seeds, wearing a saffron robe. A nomad, wandering from town to town singing for his supper playing a single stringed ektar carved from a gourd made of bamboo and goatskin. Music/song is sustenance for the Baul; a pure form of orature.

I was asked at the end of my own reading: *Is this the new experimental poetry? Are all American poets experimenting as you are? With your voice? And what about being a woman? Is this what women do?*

I had been working with texts and performance inspired by lieder and opera and by Indian raga. I was chanting "skin, meat, bones" that night. I had also begun a piece addressed to John Cage, timed to an hour. I invited others to join me—voices, instruments, with Cage's own texts collaged in for particular performances. I read my "libretto" lying underneath a piano accessing a *sprechstimme* mode, that stopped and started in fragments, moving between recitative and aria. I initiated several performances with a group of poets calling ourselves the Gertude Stein Players and we would intercut our texts with hers. And some of these pieces were entering the magnum opus that was just beginning to gestate: *The Iovis Trilogy: Colors in The Mechanism of Concealment*. This was to be a twenty-year project of more than 1,000 pages that travels around the world, in and out of forms, genres, identities, hybrid "experiment" that was also intended as a cultural intervention, challenging patriarchy, exposing the crimes of the father, of empire, capitalism. *Iovis*, the generative, active deeds: *of* Jove. It was to be a feminist epic.

Afterword

The End of Literature
Robert Coover

All thirty-three of these meditations on the nature of experimental literature in our time are thoughtful, imaginative, earnest, provocative, and many of them are, themselves, *forms* of experimental writing, clever ways to address the topic in its own language, as it were. Literature's mainstream is not a river that flows between fixed banks, but one that must be cut, and it is the experimental writer who, avoiding the backwaters of the often more lucrative and momentarily celebrated conventional writing, can be found at the cutting edge. We all know this. But what if literature itself is an expiring holdover from the last century, using an outmoded technology and fast declining into an archival state of primary interest only to scholars and hobbyists, the current worldwide proliferation of writing programs nothing but a death rattle? What if it's over, and the wildest and most brilliant of experiments won't revive it?

Some thirty-three all-too-brief centuries ago, the 13th century BCE redactor of the then-500-year-old Gilgamesh Epic, our oldest known sustained literary narrative, added a frame story which pretends to locate, hidden within a copper foundation box under the legendary ramparts of Uruk, themselves by his time long since fallen into dusty ruin, a text engraved on lapis lazuli and perhaps inscribed by Gilgamesh himself upon his return from his adventures, which presumably is the story about to be told, a modernist, if not postmodernist, metafictional contrivance right at the very beginning of what we call literature. Which at the time was itself a new experiment, so new that the author of the original Epic didn't even have an alphabet with which to compose.

Literature, etymologically "things made from letters," can be seen as a specific artistic process, containing within itself its own potential and limitations, one that began at a certain time in human intellectual history, a time when written words themselves were often believed to be sacred and magical, and a process that has evolved over the subsequent centuries, using generations of writers to fulfill itself. But for many reasons—a radical change of focus, a discontinuance of the tools including writing itself, a sense of completion or exhaustion or irrelevance, an impatience with the attention demanded, a transfer of such activity into other media less "made from letters"—such a process can come to an end.

The invention of the movie camera at the end of the 19th century and the international industrial cinema that followed had already dented print narrative's dominance—it was so hard to read a book, so easy to watch a movie—when, as the last century was winding down, along came programmable machines called computers. Whereupon human discourse began to move off the page and into the infinitely spacious digital universe, a radically divergent medium that both absorbed everything from the old technology and ultimately displaced it; print documents could be read on laptops and phone screens (and largely are now), but hypermediated sound, text, and image could not be moved into print. Only mad religionists and some wistful librarians continued to venerate the printed word.

A tool engineered to embrace and set in concerted motion, not only language, but all signs and gestures, icons, objects, sounds and images, and with instant access to global networks, has to be a powerful tool. It becomes, itself, a kind of rhetoric by which to hold the ever shape-shifting world together, and is admirably placed to play a major role in this current age of the New Sophists. In our present intellectual environment, the Platonic hierarchies left over from the Middle Ages have mostly vanished and the borders between the traditional Aristotelian disciplines and classifications established during the Enlightenment have been rapidly dissolving, leaving us all enmeshed in vast webworks of signs which ceaselessly appear and disappear, the world as Sophists have always seen it. And these signs are not merely those of traditional literacy, of alphabetical language, of text, but now include streaming sound and moving images, as well as new rhetorical elements like multilinearity, hyperlinks, kinetic and metamorphosing text, haptics, immersive virtual reality, together with a multitude of ancillary tools and apps, elements that may eventually leave the screen altogether and environ us.

Sophists live in a world of ceaseless actional and, as we would say now, informational flow—that river one steps into, never the same twice, with man, not at the center of it, just *in* it—*but*: as the measure and measurer *of* it. That is, man calls it river and so it is river, says it flows and so it does flow. For the Sophist, knowledge—which is not a given, but is created—is power, and that power is accessed, classically, through rhetoric. They invent new words and concepts and, if others adopt them, their power grows. Like Platonists, Sophists also use a kind of dialectic, though a skeptical one, without hope of synthesis, which they don't believe in. They set up dialectical oppositions and simply make choices; then, using a rhetoric aimed at persuasion, they argue for the choices they have made. The distinction between Being and Becoming is, for them, a false one. Being is what there is, and it looks just like Becoming, and anyway it's where we live, nothing we can do about it.

In this 3D installation we call the modern world, the computer is a perfect rhetorical tool. In its root-deep either-or operations, it even thinks like a Sophist. It makes visible the ceaseless flow of words and actions and offers entry points for all users to exercise their own interactive skills in an effort to exert influence and acquire power and pleasure, the initial and perhaps principal challenge being to grab people's attention out in all that turbulence and come up with a way to hang on to it; to find followers and keep them. Everything depends on information input and proper programming, and then on asking the right questions, winner take all. A game of games in which to be absent is to lose. Timing is everything. Gates and Bezos and Zuckerberg win, everyone else loses. Knowledge is power for the Sophist, and knowing is doing, but you have to move quickly, be the first with the new, and fuck the competition. Fuck the rest of the world, too, for that matter. It's a zero-sum game.

Writers, of course, do not as a rule move quickly. Most of these authors are designing poems and narrative structures that demand a lot of thought, a lot of time. It can take weeks to hammer out a decent sentence, a single line of poetry, and it can take just as long to read and fully understand those lines. Fortunes can rise and fall, regimes too, while researching a single minute narrative detail or finding the perfect prosody, the theatrically dramatic turn of phrase. The written word is a poor sluggish traveler in a high velocity time, an ancient clumsy makeshift tool, invented by people who worked in clay and moved at the speed of a camel. Information as data can now be accessed and sorted at the speed of light, but literature is not mere information, as all authors insist, and speed in the composition or processing of it has never been considered a virtue. Writing as a craft requires patience and discipline, and the same is asked of the reader. Slow down... Listen... Hardest thing in the world for today's rapid-fire multitasking user, bopping about urgently on various social media networks and researching the universe minute by minute. In the digital age, literature, written or read, is widely looked upon as a misuse of time (still precious, time is, that hasn't changed, nor likely will), its potential played out, nothing left but nuance and repetition, even as some make use of the print narrative industry for their own profit and pleasure, in the way that the author of the Gilgamesh epic and his tenured priestly and scribal friends made use of the gullibility of the illiterate for their own continued well-being.

While authors sometimes spend entire lives attempting to perfect a single poem or story, programmable machines can generate an infinite number of works, more or less instantly, and, who knows, maybe some of them are "perfect." Dartmouth College, in announcing its 2018 Literary Creative Turing Tests, offers thousand-dollar prizes each for machine-generated programs that "have the ability to produce effectively an infinite number" of sonnets, limericks, original short poems, and children's stories. The outputs of the sonnet and limerick generators are judged blindly in competition with "human" sonnets and limericks, with any poem indistinguishable from human outputs successfully passing the "Turing Test." The short poems ("literary metacreations") and children's stories are evaluated for their "artistry." All that's missing is a program to generate an infinite number of appreciative readers, though what's being "read," of course, is not the infinitude of individual poems and stories (mortal tedium, in the words of Samuel Beckett), but the limited mass of materials fed into the generator in each program, together with the combinatory patterns that the "meta-author" has designed, allowing the reader to "see" the whole, without having to suffer any of the particular outputs.

Is something being lost? Sure, it is. For one thing, the pleasure of curling up in front of the fire with a bound codex—"the haptics of the printed word," as a book-loving friend has put it. For another, the "deep read" that a book invites with its page-turning mechanism, a mechanism that allows one to go back and reread, over and over. Some say that irony was born in that peculiarity of the book. But, if nowadays there is less of the sustained readerly attention that literature has traditionally demanded, one can anticipate that new experimental forms will emerge to reach these restless rewired generations, and that writers, if in the post-literature world they are still to be called writers, will continue, in whatever medium and with whatever tools, to tell stories, explore paradox, strive for meaning and beauty (those sweet old illusions), pursue self-understanding, seek out the hidden content of the tribal life, and so on—in short, all the grand endeavors we associate with literature, even if what they make may not be literature, any more than film is literature or nature a poem.

Though literature as an art form may be fading away, however, raw storytelling seems to be part of everyman's DNA, deeper than form or distribution mode, and, as Boccaccio's plague stories remind us, will probably continue to the end of human time. Because: what else? And even if narrative and lyrical artists, whether experimental or conventional, are reduced to stand-up comedy, eulogies, rap lyrics, and tweeted epigrams, they will still feel the tug of the obligations that Hesiod laid upon the Muses a couple of millennia ago: to engage with the national rituals and dogmas, to be witnesses of their times, and to provide consolation and entertainment—or, as he put it, to make the gods laugh. Assuming you can find them, logged on and adrift in cyberspace as they are now.

o o o o o

Notes on Contributors

Mark Amerika is the author of many books, including *remixthebook* (2011) and *Locus Solus: An Inappropriate Translation Composed in a 21st Century Manner* (2014). He is a Professor of Art and Art History and Founding Director of the Doctoral Program in Intermedia Art, Writing and Performance in the new College of Media, Communication and Information at the University of Colorado Boulder.

Martine Antle holds the McCaughey Chair of French Studies at the University of Sydney. As a specialist in twentieth-century French theater, contemporary writing, photography and painting, she has published extensively on race and gender in twentieth and twenty-first century French and Francophone literature. Her scholarship spans the political, social, and cultural revolutions that shaped modernity from the turn of the twentieth century to the present.

Poet, essayist, theorist, and scholar **Charles Bernstein** is a foundational member and leading practitioner of Language poetry. He has been active in the experimental poetry scenes in New York and San Francisco, not only as a poet, but also as an editor, publisher, and theorist. His poetry combines the language of politics, popular culture, advertising, literary jargon, corporate-speak, and myriad others to show the ways in which language and culture are mutually constructive and interdependent. Bernstein has published dozens of books, including poetry and essay collections, pamphlets, translations, collaborations, and libretti. His poetry has been widely anthologized and translated, and it has appeared in over 500 magazines and periodicals.

R. M. Berry taught twentieth-century literature, critical theory, and creative writing (fiction) at Florida State University. He is the author of the novels *Frank* (2005) and *Leonardo's Horse*, a New York Times "notable book" of 1998. His first collection of short fiction, *Plane Geometry and Other Affairs of the Heart,* won the

1985 Fiction Collective prize, and his second, *Dictionary of Modern Anguish* (2000), was described by the *Buffalo News* as "a collection of widely disparate narratives inspired . . . by the spirit of Ludwig Wittgenstein." Berry's essays on experimental fiction and philosophy have appeared in *New Literary History, symplokē, Narrative, Philosophy and Literature,* the *Oxford Handbook of Philosophy and Literature,* and anthologies in the U.S., France, and Germany. He retired from teaching in 2017.

Timothy Bewes is Associate Professor of English at Brown University. He is the author of *Cynicism and Postmodernity* (1997), *Reification, or the Anxiety of Late Capitalism* (2002), and *The Event of Postcolonial Shame* (2011).

Christian Bök is the author of *Eunoia*, a bestselling work of experimental literature, which has gone on to win the Griffin Prize for Poetic Excellence. Bök is currently working on *The Xenotext*— a project that requires him to encipher a poem into the genome of a bacterium capable of surviving in any inhospitable environment. Bök is a Fellow in the Royal Society of Canada, and he teaches at Charles Darwin University.

Julie Carr is the author of six books of poetry, most recently *100 Notes on Violence* (2010), *RAG* (2014), and *Think Tank* (2015). She is also the author of *Surface Tension: Ruptural Time and the Poetics of Desire in Late Victorian Poetry* (2013), and the co-editor of *Active Romanticism: The Radical Impulse in Nineteenth-Century and Contemporary Poetic Practice* (2015). She has been the recipient of numerous awards and honors, including The Sawtooth Poetry Prize, and The National Poetry Series.

Robert Coover is a writer of avant-garde fiction, plays, poetry, and essays whose experimental forms and techniques are widely noted and praised. His work as a metafictionist has had a vast influence on a generation of postmodern writers.

Jeffrey DeShell has published six novels, most recently *Arthouse* (2011) and *Expectation* (2013), some art criticism, and a critical book of Poe's fiction. He was a Fulbright Teaching Fellow in Budapest, and has taught in Northern Cyprus, the American Midwest and Bard College. Currently he's a professor at the University of Colorado Boulder, where he lives with the novelist Elisabeth Sheffield and their two children.

Jeffrey R. Di Leo is Dean of the School of Arts & Sciences and Professor of English and Philosophy at the University of Houston-Victoria. He is editor and publisher of *American Book Review*, and the founder and editor of *symplokē*. His books include *Fiction's Present: Situating Contemporary Narrative Innovation* (2008, with R. M. Berry), *Federman's Fictions: Innovation, Theory, and the Holocaust* (2011), *Turning the Page: Book Culture in the Digital Age* (2014), *Criticism after Critique: Aesthetics, Literature, and the Political* (2014), *Dead Theory: Derrida, Death, and the Afterlife of Theory* (2015), *Higher Education under Late Capitalism: Identity, Conduct, and the Neoliberal Condition* (2016), *American Literature as World Literature* (2017), and the *Bloomsbury Handbook of Literary and Cultural Theory* (2018).

The author of nine novels, three collections of short fiction, two books of essays and five books of poetry, **Rikki Ducornet** has received both a Lannan Literary Fellowship and the Lannan Literary Award For Fiction. She has received the Bard College Arts and Letters award and, in 2008, an Academy Award in Literature. Her work is widely published abroad. Recent exhibitions of her paintings include the solo show *Desirous* at the Pierre Menard Gallery in Cambridge, Massachusetts, in 2007, and the group shows: *O Reverso Do Olhar* in Coimbra, Portugal, in 2008, and *El Umbral Secreto* at the Museo de la Solidaridad Salvador Allende in Santiago, Chile, in 2009. She has illustrated books by Jorge Luis Borges, Robert Coover, Forest Gander, Kate Bernheimer, Joanna Howard and Anne Waldman among others. Her collected papers including prints and drawings are in the permanent collection of the Ohio State University Rare Books and Manuscripts Library. Her work is in the permanent collections of the Museo de la Solidaridad Salvador Allende, Santiago, Chile, The McMaster University Museum, Ontario, Canada, and The

Bibliothèque Nationale, Paris.

Brian Evenson is the author of a dozen books of fiction, most recently the story collection *A Collapse of Horses* (2016) and the novella *The Warren* (2016). Other recent publications include *Windeye* (2012) and *Immobility* (2012). He lives in Los Angeles and teaches in the Critical Studies Program at CalArts.

Douglas Glover is an itinerant Canadian writer, author of four novels, five story collections and three books of nonfiction. His novel *Elle* won the Governor General's Award for Fiction in 2003. He was publisher and editor of the online magazine *Numéro Cinq* (2010-2017).

Kenneth Goldsmith is the author of ten books of poetry, the founding editor of the online archive UbuWeb, and a senior editor of PennSound, an archive of online poetry housed at the University of Pennsylvania, where he also teaches English and Creative Writing.

Laird Hunt was born in Singapore and has lived in London, The Hague, Tokyo, Strasbourg, Paris and New York. A former United Nations Press Officer whose essays and reviews have been published in the *New York Times*, the *Washington Post*, the *Wall Street Journal*, the *Guardian* and elsewhere, he is the author of several novels including *Kind One* (2012), *Neverhome* (2014) and *In the House in the Dark of the Woods* (2018).

Jacques Jouet writes poetry, short stories, novels, theater, and essays. He has been a member of the Oulipo (Ouvroir de Littérature Potentielle) since 1983. His most recent publications are: *Du jour* (2013), *La scène est sur la scène, théâtre complet* (pol.editeur.com), *Le Cocommuniste* (2014), and *Ruminations du potentiel* (2016).

Julie Larios is the recipient of an Academy of American Poets Prize, a Pushcart Prize for Poetry, and a Washington State Arts Commission/Artist Trust Fellowship. She recently retired from the faculty of The Vermont College of Fine Art and currently lives in Bellingham, Washington, about ninety miles north of Seattle and forty-seven miles south of Vancouver, B.C.

Daniel Levin Becker is literary editor of *The Believer* and a member of the Oulipo. His first book, *Many Subtle Channels: In Praise of Potential Literature*, was published by Harvard University Press in 2012.

Mark Lipovetsky was born in Sverdlovsk (currently Ekaterinburg, Russia), where he graduated from the university and defended two dissertations. He moved to the United States in 1996, and he teaches at the University of Colorado Boulder. He is the author of more than a hundred articles published in the US, Russia, and Europe, nine books, and co-editor of twelve volumes on Russian literature and culture.

Michael Martone teaches in the English Department at the University of Alabama. His most recent books include *Winesburg, Indiana* (2016); *Memoranda* (2016); and *Four for a Quarter: Fictions* (2011). *Brooding*, a book of essays, will be published in 2018 by the University of Georgia Press.

Carole Maso is the author of ten books, including the novels *The Art Lover* (1990), *Ava* (1993), *Defiance* (1998) and *Mother & Child* (2012); poems in prose, *Aureole* (1969) and *Beauty is Convulsive* (2011); essays, *Break Every Rule* (2000), and a journal of pregnancy and birth, *The Room Lit by Roses* (2000). She is Professor of Literary Arts at Brown University.

A critic, poet, and professor, **Steve McCaffery** was part of the Canadian avant-garde poetry scene in the 1970s. His creative work has been marked by innovation and a move away from conventionally narrative forms. His oeuvre includes sound poetry (as part of the collaborative group the Four Horsemen with poets Rafael Barreto-Rivera, Paul Dutton, and bpNichol) and concrete poetry. His visual poetry is in permanent collections at the National Gallery of Canada in Ottawa, the Paul Getty Research Institute in

Malibu, the International Concrete Poetry Archive in Oxford, England, and the New York Public Library in New York City.

Christina Milletti teaches in the Department of English at SUNY Buffalo. Her fiction has appeared in a variety of journals and anthologies, such as *The Iowa Review, The Cincinnati Review, Denver Quarterly, The Master's Review,* and *Harcourt's Best New American Voices.* She has just finished a new collection called *Girling Seasons* and is now working on a novel about Cuba.

Ian Monk is a British writer and translator, based in Paris. He writes in both English and French, and he translates in both directions. He has been a member of the Oulipo since 1998. He won the Scott Moncrieff Prize in 2004 for his transation of Daniel Pennac's *Monsieur Malaussène.*

Warren Motte is College Professor of Distinction at the University of Colorado Boulder. He specializes in contemporary French literature, with particular focus upon experimentalist works that put accepted notions of literary form into question. His most recent books include *Fables of the Novel: French Fiction since 1990* (2003), *Fiction Now: The French Novel in the Twenty-First Century* (2008), *Mirror Gazing* (2014), and *French Fiction Today* (2017).

Doug Nufer writes fiction and poetry based on formal constraints. His recent books include *Lounge Acts* (2013), *Lifeline Rule* (2015) and *The Me Theme* (2017).

Lance Olsen is a writer known for his experimental, lyrical, fragmentary, cross-genre narratives that question the limits of historical knowledge. Since 2007 he has taught experimental narrative theory and practice at the University of Utah, and since 2002 he has served as Chair of the Board of Directors at Fiction Collective Two, one of America's best-known ongoing literary experiments and progressive art communities.

Vanessa Place was the first poet to perform as part of the Whitney Biennial; a content advisory was posted. Exhibition work has appeared at MAK Center/Schindler House; Denver Museum of Contemporary Art; the Boulder Museum of Contemporary Art; The Power Plant, Toronto; the Broad Museum, East Lansing; Various Small Fires, Los Angeles; and Cage 83 Gallery, New York. Selected recent performance venues include Museum of Modern Art, New York; Museum of Contemporary Art, Los Angeles; Detroit Museum of Contemporary Art; Mestno Musej, Ljubljana; Swiss Institute, New York; the Kitchen, New York; Andre Bely Center, St. Petersburg, Russia; Kunstverein, Cologne; Whitechapel Gallery, London; Frye Art Museum, Seattle; the Sorbonne; and De Young Museum, San Francisco. Books include *Boycott*; *Statement of Facts*; *La Medusa*; *Dies: A Sentence*; *The Guilt Project: Rape, Morality, and Law*; *Notes on Conceptualisms*, co-authored with Robert Fitterman; her translations from the French of *Guantanamo* (poetry, Frank Smith) and *Image-Material* (art theory, Dominique Peysson); and her art-audio book, *Last Words*. Place also works as a criminal defense attorney.

Gerald Prince is Professor of Romance Languages at the University of Pennsylvania. He is the author of several books, including *A Dictionary of Narratology* (1987), *Narrative as Theme* (1992), and *Guide du roman de langue française: 1901-1950* (2002). In 2013 he received the Wayne C. Booth Lifetime Achievement Award from the International Society for the Study of Narrative.

Brian Quinn is an Assistant Professor of French at the University of Colorado Boulder, where he teaches classes on Sub-Saharan Francophone African literature and culture. His research focuses on theatrical forms and stage practices in Senegal from colonial times to the present.

Eleni Sikelianos is the author of eight books of poetry, most recently *Make Yourself Happy*, from which part of this essay was drawn, as well as two hybrid memoirs (*The Book of Jon* and *You*

Animal Machine). As a translator, she has published Jacques Roubaud's *Exchanges on Light* (2006) and Sabine Macher's *The L Notebook* (2014). She has recently joined the Literary Arts Faculty at Brown University.

Alan Singer teaches in the Department of English at Temple University. He works in the field of literary aesthetics and literary theory, and he writes on aesthetic issues in literature and in the visual arts. He has published five critical books, most recently *The Self-Deceiving Muse: Notice and Knowledge in the Work of Art* (2010). His new book, *Posing Sex: Toward a Perceptual Ethics for Literary and Visual Art*, was published in 2018 by Bloomsbury. He is also a novelist. His most recent work of fiction is *The Inquisitor's Tongue* (2012).

Cole Swensen is the author of sixteen collections of poetry and a volume of critical essays; various books have won the Iowa Poetry Prize, the S.F. State Poetry Center Book Award, and the National Poetry Series, while others have been finalists for the National Book Award and the Los Angeles Times Book Award. Also a translator, she has received the PEN USA Award in Literary Translation. She teaches at Brown University. www.coleswensen. com.

Steve Tomasula is the author of the novels *The Book of Portraiture* (2006), *VAS: An Opera in Flatland* (2003), *TOC: A New-Media Novel* (2010), and *IN&OZ* (2012). He is also the author of a collection of short fiction entitled *Once Human: Stories* (2014). He teaches in the Department of English at the University of Notre Dame.

Naomi Toth teaches English literature at the Université Paris Nanterre. She is the author of *L'Écriture vive: Woolf, Sarraute, une autre phénoménologie de la perception* (2016) and has co-edited article collections on emotion in literature and the arts, and on the translation of sound in Proust. *After Vanessa Place*, an email exchange with the poet, was published as an art book by Ma Bibliothèque in 2017.

Internationally recognized and acclaimed poet **Anne Waldman** has been an active member of the "Outrider" experimental poetry community, a culture she has helped create and nurture for over four decades as writer, editor, teacher, performer, magpie scholar, infra-structure curator, and cultural/political activist. Her poetry is recognized in the lineages of the Beat, New York School, and Black Mountain trajectories of the New American Poetry. She is a founder of The Poetry Project at St Mark's Church In-the-Bowery and the Jack Kerouac School, Naropa University in Boulder, Colorado. She is the author most recently of *Gossamurmur* (2013), *Voice's Daughter of A Heart Yet To Be Born* (2016), and *Trickster Feminism* (2018), and co-editor of the anthology *CROSS WORLDS: Transcultural Poetics* (2014).

A Checklist of JEF Titles

* Winners of the Kenneth Patchen Award for the Innovative Novel

Made in the USA
Monee, IL
17 January 2021

57859881R00154